Alberto Ascari

The First Double World Champion

Copyright © CHRONOSPORTS S.A., 2004

Jordils Park,
Rue des Jordils 40,
CH-1025 St-Sulpice,
SWITZERLAND
Tel.: +41 (0)21 694 24 44
Fax: +41 (0)21 694 24 46
E-mail: info@chronosports.com
www.chronosports.com

Printing in France by Imprimerie Clerc.
Bound in France by S.I.R.C.
Photo engraving done in Switzerland by Actual Sàrl.

ISBN 2-84707-064-8

Alberto Ascari
The First Double World Champion

by

Pierre Ménard and Jacques Vassal

English version translated and edited by
David Waldron

Illustrations
Pierre Ménard

Photographs
LAT (unless otherwise stated)

Coordination
Cyril Davillerd

Dummy
Cyril Davillerd

Layout
Cyril Davillerd, Solange Amara, Désirée Ianovici

Contents

Alberto ASCARI

Chapter 1
1950 and before
Forza Italia!

In early days of their Empire the Romans built the first paved roads for political, military and economic reasons. Along them rolled wagons, carriages, horses, herds and troops criss-crossing Italy from Rome to the south and then to the north in the direction of Gaul and other colonies. Names like via Appia, Aprillia, Aurelia, Flaminia, Fulvia strike a chord in the minds of the modern day motorist. They became the tarred roads of the twentieth century and one of the major Turin based manufacturers, Lancia, adopted them as names for some of the most famous models in its range between 1950 and 1970 after which it went back to using letters from the Greek alphabet (Delta, Dedra and Kappa) as had been the case in the 20s and 30s (Lambda and Kappa).

Routes are often traced by military conquest and for political unification something that took a further fourteen centuries in Italy after the fall of the Roman Empire in 476 AD. The conquest by the Lombards under Albion (568 AD) left deep and long-lasting scars as he occupied almost the whole of the Po and Piedmont plains and sowed the seeds of an insidious and enduring antagonism between Milan and Turin, capitals of Lombardy and Piedmont respectively which, today, have become cultural and industrial centres. One is the home of Alfa Romeo and the other of Fiat and Lancia, and they have both had a long-time involvement in motor racing. Antonio Ascari and his son Alberto came from the Lombardy capital.

Over the Saxon and Carolingian eras papal power gradually established itself as the only stable political element in Italian society, which was frequently torn apart either by internal wars like that of Guelfis (papists) against Gibelins (lackeys of the Romano-German Empire) in the XIIIth and XIVth centuries, the Florentine struggles and of course the French invasion followed by Spanish domination in the XVIth century. Then for part of the XIXth century the country was shared between the French and Austrians. Present-day Italy was born in 1848 a year of civil war in Sicily, Tuscany, Naples and Lombardy whose aim was to liberate the country from the Austro-French yoke and found a republic. Before this the country was under the control of Napoleon who had created the kingdom of Italy in 1805 and had himself crowned king in Naples that same year while giving his brothers the title of viceroys. This era only lasted until 1814 and was instrumental in creating the "Risorgimento" a movement for unification based on an upsurge of nationalistic sentiment. After Giuseppe Mazzini, the theorist of the 1830s and founder of the "Young Italy" movement came Garibaldi who conquered the kingdom of Naples, which he then persuaded to join the newborn Italy. However, the man responsible for putting all the pieces of the jigsaw together was Cavour, the cunning Piedmontaise politician and minister of King Victor-Emmanuel II. With the help of the French the Piedmontaise army conquered the Austrians in 1859 and in 1861, the year of Cavour's death,

the first Italian parliament met in Turin. Florence became the capital of the new kingdom reigned over by Victor-Emmanuel II and then in 1870, thanks to the fall of the Second Empire in France, the seat of power moved to Rome (where Mazzini had proclaimed the Republic in 1849). In the holy city secular power finally supplanted that of the Vatican the last state to join the united Italy.

As the century neared its end the country began to develop economically, socially and culturally with the odd hiccup here and there. From 1890 onwards industry really took off producing bicycles, tricycles and then motor bikes thanks to companies like Bianchi founded in 1895 in Milan plus the first vehicles created by the young Ettore Bugatti born in the same town in 1881. In 1907, the French make Darracq set up a subsidiary which went broke two years later and was bought up by a group of Milan industrialists who created the "Anonima Lombardica Fabrica di Automobili" or A.L.F.A for short. In Turin the Ceirano, Itala, SCAT and Züst companies were absorbed one after the other by Giovanni Agnelli's F.I.A.T group founded in 1899. Felice Nazzaro was the first works driver and won several races in 1907 including the Targa Florio (held in Sicily), the Imperial Prize (on the Taunus circuit in Germany) and the A.C.F Grand Prix in Dieppe. Nazzaro went on to build his own cars as did his team-mate Vincenzo Lancia (2nd in the 1907 Targa Florio) whose vehicles were to achieve lasting fame. They were among the early driver/constructors long before Jack Brabham and Bruce McLaren.

The first railway line was inaugurated between Genoa and Turin when Italy was reunified. As the 20th century dawned trains linked Rome, Naples and Milan. The invention of the motor car plus the modernisation of the road network increased the mobility of the population especially to the North as the south called the "Mezzogiorno" consisted mainly of peasant small holdings dominated by a decadent aristocracy, and lagged way behind the rest of the country in terms of industrialisation. In the 20s this resulted in a huge migration from the south to the north as well as abroad to countries like France, Belgium, Great Britain, the USA and Germany.

Culturally speaking Italy's glorious Renaissance past, whose renown had spread worldwide thanks to Tuscany and its architecture in particular (the palaces and museums of Florence and Sienna) painters like Leonardo da Vinci, Piero della Francesca, political philosophy (Machiavelli) and the poetry of Dante and Petrarh, was but a distant memory. The XVIIth century saw a musical rebirth thanks to Claudio Monteverdi (1567-1643) followed by Antonio Vivaldi (1678-1741) in the XVIIIth and the Tuscan Luigi Boccherini (born in Luques in 1743). Between 1860 and 1910 a new generation of artists contributed to Italy's greatness among them painters like Modigliani, Morandi, De Chirico plus writers like de Carducci and d'Annunzio and in the realm of opera Verdi and Puccini. In this context it is worth noting that the famous Milan opera house exercised a real fascination for racing drivers. Enzo Ferrari always said that he would have liked to have been an opera singer and Giuseppe Campari, one of his Alfa Romeo drivers and Antonio Ascari's great friend, was an excellent baritone. Later on Phil Hill, another Ferrari driver also fell under the spell of La Scala.

Italy was a constitutional monarchy with right wing prime ministers up to 1876 and then left-wingers until 1900. The second king Humbert 1st was assassinated in 1900 and as neither he nor his successor Victor-Emmanuel III did anything to improve the lot of the workers and peasant there were numerous strikes. In 1911-12 Italy waged war against Turkey and the result was the annexation of Tripoli and the Dardanelles. These successes encouraged politicians and public opinion to embark upon reconquering home territories that had once been part of the Austro-Hungarian Empire, and one of the consequences of this was that Italy entered WWI on the side of the Allies. Like everywhere else in Europe the result was a very high death toll and a large amount of damage, which left behind a malaise that infected a whole generation as shown in the excellent film "Men Against" directed by Francesco Rosi with Gian Maria Volonte. The poet Gabriele d'Annunzio (born in Pescara in 1868) already famous for his works like "The Child of Pleasure" in 1889 and "Fire" in 1900 came back from the war cultivating an elitist dandy-like stance and a certain taste for risk by flying a plane. When peace broke out he drove sports Alfa Romeos like Blaise Cendrars, a French poet of Swiss origins. Later on d'Annunzio became a political adventurer and an ally of the fascist regime. Despite the workers' struggles in which communists and anarchists played a role and the growing membership of the Communist Party founded by Ugo Togliatti and Antonio Gramsci, it was a cunning former socialist teacher and demagogue, Benito Mussolini, who best exploited Italy's post-war frustrations as all it had gained from the 1919 Saint-German-en-Laye

treaty were the regions of Haut-Adige, Trentino and Fiume. Mussolini became a minister in 1922 after his famous march on Rome, and relying on the support of his nationalistic black-shirted fascist party in which young people were enrolled either voluntary or by force proclaimed himself "Duce" in 1925. He was a lover of cars and motor bikes and very quickly understood the political advantages to be gained from sport in general and motor sport in particular. He backed the creation of road events, praised the racing successes of makes like Alfa Romeo and Maserati and promoted the careers of drivers like Nuvolari and Varzi who were at the height of their glory in the 30s. It was thus no coincidence that the

• **3**_ Long Island 24th October 1906: Vincenzo Lancia in his FIAT finishes second in the Vanderbilt Cup behind Louis Wagner's Darracq.

• **4**_ 27th April 1907: Felice Nazzaro in his FIAT just before the start of the Targa Florio which he won. Together with Giovani Agnelli he was one of the founders of the Turin Company in 1899 after which he became one of the greatest drivers of his era.

• **5 and 6_** Dieppe 6th July 1907: Felice Nazzaro and the men from FIAT at the weigh-in for the ACF Grand Prix. The winning FIAT had a twin-block 16,286 cc 4-cylinder engine that put out 130 bhp at 1600 rpm and was capable of reaching 160 km/h!

famous Mille Miglia was held for the first time in 1927 in a party-like atmosphere. Then came the Tripoli Grand Prix in the 30s endowed with huge sums of prize money and also the scene of sumptuous extravagance. Libya had been colonised by Italy in 1911 and in 1935-36 Mussolini's troops conquered Ethiopia as part of "Il Duce's" plans for an African empire. In 1936

the Italian army lent a hand to Franco's forces against those of the Republicans in the Spanish Civil War as well as the German aviation (the bombing of Guernica in 1937). This was the highly explosive political atmosphere in which the young Alberto Ascari began his racing career, which we will return to shortly.

Motor racing was suspended when Italy entered WWII on Germany's side, a decision that was to cost a whole generation dear thanks to the latter's occupation and Allied bombing at the time of the liberation (invasion of Sicily and the battle of Monte Casino). After Mussolini's death in 1945 the reconstruction of the country began both politically and economically. In 1946, Italy was declared a republic following a referendum. This was really the beginning of the country's modern era, which was greatly helped by the American aid it received thanks to the Marshal Plan. The Christian Democrats led by De Gasperi were in power up to 1953 and began Italy's reconstruction. There was plenty of work about as factories, railways, the whole infrastructure and services had to be rebuilt. Salaries, though, were minimal which led to a series of very tough and long-lasting strikes that also affected the car industry. However, it was a period in which Turin-based Lancia and Fiat brought out new models - the Aurelia and the 1400 - which sold very well. In Maranello near Modena – home of Maserati - Ferrari created his famous make (1947) and in Milan Alfa Romeo, whose Alfettas were harvesting victories in the post-war Grands Prix, was about to launch its first road-going cars starting with the 1900 in 1951 and then the Giulietta in 1955. In the 50s the stirrings of the "Dolce Vita" aspect of Italian society were portrayed in the cinema thanks to stars like Marcello Mastroianni and Sophia Loren despite the social injustices and the influence of an ultra-conservative clergy plus political instability up to 1958 after which the Christian Democrats returned to power for ten years. Revolt and hope in Italian society were expressed by film makers like Roberto Rossellini (Rome, Open City in 1945), Federico Fellini (La Strada 1946) writers such as Malaparte ("Skin" 1947) Alberto Moravia ("Boredom") the poems and essays of Cesare Pavese who committed suicide in Turin in 1950. A little later Pier Paolo Pasolini (The Gramsci Ashes 1957) was part of a new generation of film makers succeeding Visconti, Fellini and Antonioni which included Ettore Scola, the Taviani brothers and Marco Ferreri (1).*

Urban development exploded and cities like Naples fell prey to chaotic expansion leading to increasing traffic jams and the streets were invaded by hordes of buzzing Vespas and Lambrettas, a fashion which caught on in France and other countries and helped to improve Italy's balance of payments! This too was the era of very small cars like the Fiat 500 and 600, the Isetta and Vespa 400. In addition to singers and film stars certain sportsmen became popular heroes: motorbike rider Carlo Ubbiali, cyclist Fausto Coppi (il campionissimo) and of course Alberto Ascari who seemed destined for greatness given his background, as his father Antonio had been one of Italy's pre-WWII stars so a brief sketch of his career follows. ∎

(1) * Roberto Rossellini was one of the links between the cinema and motor racing as he was a regular Ferrari client and raced in the 1953 Mille Miglia in an open 250 MM Viginale stopping in Rome where a terrified Ingrid Bergman implored him to retire. In his film Amarcord Fellini also depicted the passage of the Mille Miglia through in his home town of Rimini when he was a child.

• 7_ Palermo 11ᵗʰ May 1913: Felice Nazzaro before the start of the Targa Florio which he won at the wheel of a car bearing his own name.

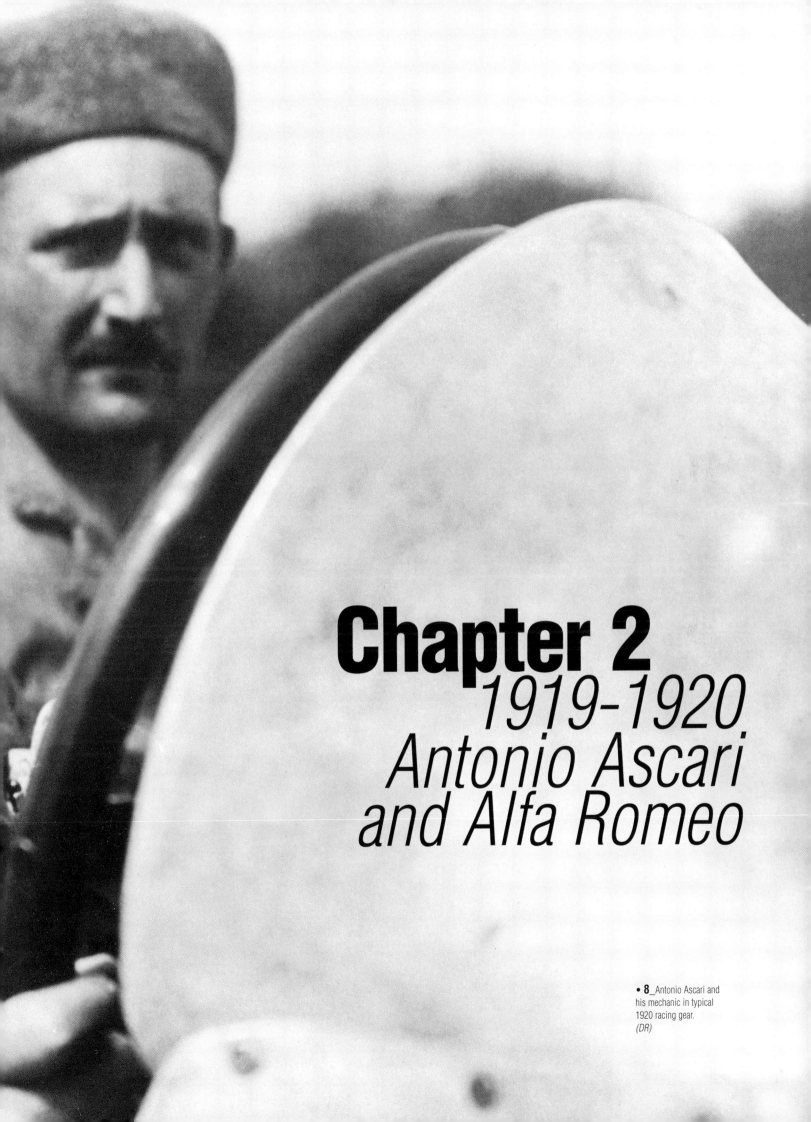

Chapter 2
1919-1920
Antonio Ascari
and Alfa Romeo

● **8**_Antonio Ascari and
his mechanic in typical
1920 racing gear.
(DR)

"Antonio had a strong character and was an exceptionally active and courageous man. He went to Brazil with two of his brothers to build a narrow gauge railway and was also an ideal father and husband and great company. When you were with him there was no way you could pay as he was generous to a fault and whenever necessary he knew how to act with humility. Although he had left school early he was extremely cultivated and when he found himself faced with a technical problem he couldn't solve he never hesitated to ask advice from people he thought knew more than he did." [1]

This is how Enzo Ferrari described Antonio Ascari, Alberto's father, and one of the great drivers of the 20s in his memoirs. Antonio was born in Castel d'Ario in the Mantua region in 1887. His father sold seeds and among his clients was a farmer called Nuvolari who was, in fact, Tazio's father, the legendary "campionissimo' born in 1892. After winning many championship titles on motor bikes he became one of the greatest racing drivers of all time. As both lived in Mantua there is no doubt that Tazio knew Antonio even if they never raced against each other.

In contrast to Nuvolari's father Antonio's did not stay in Mantua: he went off to settle in Milan with his family (three sons and a daughter). When Antonio came back from Brazil he began selling cars and opened a garage at 60 Corso Sampione. He was immediately bitten by the racing bug and began competing in a modified 1914 4.5 litres Grand Prix FIAT. The international 4.5 litres formula (precursor of modern F1) had resulted in an extraordinary ACF Grand Prix on the Lyon circuit in 1914. The race, won by the Mercedes team, which beat the Peugeots and Delages among others, has engraved itself in racing history because of the duel opposing French and German drivers and manufacturers as in addition to Mercedes Opel also entered. Other makes included the British Vauxhalls and Sunbeams, Piccard-Pictet from Switzerland and Italy was represented by Nazzaro, Aquila Italiana and FIAT. The 1914 FIATs were among the very first cars to have 4-wheel brakes and were powered by long stroke (bore 100 mm x stroke 143 mm) monoblock engines giving a cubic capacity of 4492 ccs. Like the Bugattis of the era the car had S.O.H.C distribution and 3 valves per

(1) - "Piloti, che gente" See bibliography at the end of the book.

cylinder (1 admission and 2 exhaust) and its power output was 135 bhp at 3000 rpm. These cars had a top speed of 145 km/h and in his modified version Antonio Ascari won his first event, the Parma-Poggio di Berceto hill climb on 5th October 1919.

In this immediate post WWI period Italy was going through a very troubled political and economic period with battles between nationalists and socialists. The national debt was out of control and there were frequent strikes in both the private and public sectors. On 10th September 1919 a treaty was signed between the Italian and Austrian governments, which gave Fiume free status and Italy received Trentino, South Tyrol and Trieste. The writer Gabriele d'Annunzio, an officer during the war and a fervent nationalist, wrote to his friend Mussolini that he was launching an expedition to recapture Fiume! He set off at the head of a detachment of fewer than 300 soldiers, called "The Legionnaires," who had rallied to his cause and made a triumphant entry into Fiume. On 29th September the king decided to dissolve parliament and call general elections for 16th November. The hill climb

was thus held in total confusion, as the organisers feared the wrath of the crowd if it were cancelled.

A passion for this form of motor sport then gripped the whole of Italy. The Parma event in Poggio di Berceto created in 1913 as part of the celebrations of the 100th anniversary of Verdi's birth enjoyed the same prestige as Mont Ventoux in France. It was won by Giovanni Marsaglia in his 35-50 hp Aquila at a speed of 73.650 km/h. In 1914, victory fell to Ernesto Ceirano in a SCAT at 78.295 km/h. Then war intervened. The hill climb was revived in 1919 and was the first motor racing event in Italy since the outbreak of WWI. Thousands of spectators from Emilia, Liguria, Lombardy and Piedmont lined the route. It was run over a distance of 50,9 kms and resembled a modern-day rally special with numerous corners and a muddy surface in many places. The first section was slightly uphill followed by a downhill portion and then the road rose steeply upwards again. In two places the drivers and riding mechanics had to cross tramways. A total of thirty-eight vehicles turned up, all private entries, as the companies had agreed not to enter any works cars. The well-known driver, Ferdinando Minoia, entered his FIAT and was asked to withdraw on the eve of the hill climb. Which he did, unwillingly. It is probable, however, that several privateers benefited from a bit of behind-the-scenes help from the factories with the latter either supplying or tuning a car even if several, like Ascari's FIAT, were pre-war models. Antonio set the fastest time of the day in the third category where his rivals consisted of two Nazzaros, two Alfa Romeos, a FIAT and five Aquilas. His time of 38m 11.5s, a speed of 83.275 km/h, beat the former record. Monday's "Gazetto dello Sport" devoted a long article to the previous day's hill climb and featured a portrait of Ascari (31 years old) plus one of his main rivals 25-year-old Guido Meregalli in his Nazzaro. The paper made the following comment about Ascari: "He has a calm, serene face; almost American in fact. He is energetic and well mannered and loves cars. On first acquaintance he does not look like the champion he is and does not behave like one either. He is slightly ironic. When he gets behind the wheel he is like a man transformed: his eyes shine, his pulse is regular but he stays calm despite his audacious appearance. He lived in the United States for a time and comes from Milan."

A pointer to the future in this same hill climb was the entry in the second category of a young 21-year-old debutant driver from the same Emilia Romagna region, Enzo Ferrari. The future constructor was at the wheel of a 15/20 sports 2.3 litres 4-cylinder CMN whose top speed did not exceed 80 km/h. He finished eleventh overall and fourth in his category with a time of 50m 13.5s. The CMN company (Costruzione Meccanicha Nazionale) had just been created in Milan and Ferrari, who had been turned down by FIAT, bought a car from the fledgling firm after negotiating a special price, in order to race. Enzo became friendly with a driver, a former cyclist Ugo Sivocci, who was already with CMN. The company sent both of them to race in the Targa Florio in Sicily on 23rd November on the Madonies circuit. In the meantime Ascari raced in the Coppa della Consuma on 26th October which he won outright in his 1914 FIAT ahead of Meregalli's Nazzaro. Then he got down to preparing for the Targa Florio.

The elections on 16th November led to an overwhelming victory for the socialist and "populari" parties while the fascists did not gain a single seat. Their leader, Benito Mussolini, was so discouraged that he thought about quitting politics. Neither Ferrari nor Ascari had any inkling that very soon he would grab power by force and then begin to take a close interest in motor sport because of the sway it held over the Italians.

The Targa Florio was created in 1906 by Vincenzo Florio, son of a big building contractor, who spent a fortune on the event. It was run over a very twisty road circuit that was initially 149 kms long and went through numerous villages, which added to its charm and danger. Florio loved his native Sicily deeply and wanted the Targa to become a means of attracting tourists from the mainland and abroad. On the restart in 1919 a new, shorter 108 km circuit was used. Even so it had almost one thousand corners and was extremely tough on drivers. Repairs to the road surface could not be carried out in time so the route was pitted with potholes, gulleys etc. However, concrete pits - not wood as elsewhere – and covered stands on the start/finish straight plus a village to welcome sportsmen, drivers and spectators were built which underlined Florio's desire to make his event a permanent fixture on the calendar. There were twenty-four starters, mainly Italian (Alfa Romeo, Aquilla, CMN, Diatto, FIAT, Itala. Lancia, Nazzaro) plus a couple of French makes (Ballot and Peugeot) and English

DOPO LE GRANDI VITTORIE DELL'ANNATA

PARMA - POGGIO DI BERCETO
E CIRCUITO DEL MUGELLO

ALFA-ROMEO

su Pneumatici Pirelli

TRIONFA NUOVAMENTE nella

TARGAFLORIO

con FERRARI ENZO PRIMO della SUA CATEGORIA
SECONDO della CLASSIFICA GENERALE

(Eric-Campbell). The driver line-up included Giulio Masetti, René Thomas and André Boillot. Overall it was a quality field but given the small number of cars it looked like being a lean day for spectators. The majority of drivers had reconnoitred the circuit in touring and then racing cars (a tradition that would last a long time). The French arrived two weeks before the race to give themselves ample time to get to know the layout. During practice a violent storm hit the region followed by hailstones in the night. On race day it was pouring rain in certain places which, allied to a strong wind, meant that grip and visibility changed from one moment to the next. At 7h00 on Sunday morning the cars were flagged off from Cerda one by one at 3-minute intervals for a 4-lap race, some 432 kms. Spectators could bet on the result right up to the start of the first car! In many places the road was little better than a muddy track. Ascari shot off determined to beat Thomas's Ballot and the Peugeots (Indianapolis models) driven by Boillot and Reville plus the quickest Italians like Campari in his Alfa Romeo. By the 31-kilometre mark he had set the best time overall, 37 minutes, three faster than Thomas. Unfortunately, he came into a corner too quickly, skidded and ended up in a ditch. Campari, who was just behind, saw the driver and his mechanic thrown out of the car and then get up. They were treated a little later in the hospital for minor injuries. By the end of the race cars and drivers were covered in mud and the winner was André Boillot in his Peugeot despite stiff opposition from Thomas's Ballot. The Italian cars were never in the hunt and suffered a humiliating defeat on home territory!

Antonio Ascari's garage now at 4 Via Castelvetro in Milan had become the main Alfa Romeo dealership for Lombardy and in1920, the company hired him as one of their drivers. His season got off to a bad start: he was the provisional holder of the "Coppa Challenge" due to his win in 1919 in the Parma-Poggia di Berceto hill climb and his aim was to score a second

victory which, according to the rules, would make the trophy his. He turned up half-an-hour too late to hand in his entry form to the U.C.A.M (the Union of Cyclists and Car Drivers of Milan), as the closing date was 20h00 on 28th May for the hill climb on 30th May. The organisers proved inflexible even if it meant losing a well-known driver. So Ascari attended the event as a simple spectator. This time Enzo Ferrari took part in an Isotta-Fraschini IM, one of which had raced at Indianapolis in 1914 without exactly setting the track on fire! Thanks to its 130 bhp engine Ferrari hoped for better things than the previous year in the underpowered CMN. His main rivals for victory were Meregalli in his Nazzaro, Campari's Alfa Romeo and Count Carlo Masetti (Guilio's brother) in Ascari's FIAT. Victory went to Campari in 40m 59.45s, an improvement of over ten minutes on his previous year's time despite not having the right tyres. Into second came Masetti only 3.35s behind the burly Giuseppe. Thus, Ascari's record remained unbeaten.

The next major event was a 6-lap race on the 64 km Mugello circuit in Tuscany on 13th June. An earthquake had just hit the region and the ticket price of 500 liras was pretty steep when one thinks that bread cost 1.50 lira per kilo. Part of the gate was destined to help the victims of the disaster and in addition, substantial amounts of prize money plus cups and shields were awarded to the drivers. It was the first race on the Mugello circuit since 1914 and a big crowd turned up causing huge traffic jams. There were twenty-four entries with an interval of several minutes between each starter as in the Targa Florio. Ascari crashed on the first lap injuring himself and his mechanic. Campari notched up another win as Masetti, who was in the lead, crashed on lap 5 in the Futa downhill section (it would later become part of the Mille Miglia but covered in the opposite direction) leaving the Alfa Romeo driver with no real opposition. After making a good start Enzo Ferrari retired and only five cars were officially classified.

The Coppa della Consuma, a 16-km hill climb was held on 16th June in the Pennines and again Ascari came out empty-handed. It was a year of social and political crisis in Italy and the FIAT factories in Turin were occupied by indignant workers protesting about the night shift times. The same thing happened in the Alfa Romeo factory in Milan which closed on 30th August. In two days red flags floated over one hundred and sixty firms in the town. This was around the time when Enzo Ferrari arrived at Alfa Romeo. He was designated as one of the three works drivers for the Targa Florio scheduled for September. Finally, the event was put back until 24th October because of a dispute between the organisers and French drivers and constructors who did not turn up!

Meregalli in his Nazzaro won the race from Ferrari's Alfa Romeo. No explanation has been given as to why Ascari was not part of the Milan firm's line-up. There was still one event to go before the end of the year, the Gallarate flying kilometre in Lombardy on 14th November. It was a sprint which was very popular in the 20s as it was an excellent means of assessing the performance of various cars. Sports and touring cars each had their own category and naturally the highest speeds were set in the racing section. Ferrari was at the wheel of a Type 40/60 Alfa Romeo while Ascari had the brand new but less powerful 1921 20/30 ES Sport. Campari was entered in the 4.5 litres class. Enzo Ferrari's best was 120 km/h while Ascari hustled his Alfa through the flying kilometre at 108 km/h. The press gave much more coverage to the Alfa Romeo double as well as Campari's achievement (126,760 km/h) than the highest speed of the day set by Silvani's 12-cylinder Packard at 157.894 km/h. In his memoirs Enzo Ferrari wrote that his love of 12-cylinder engines dated from that day as the Packard's performance made a big impact on him. Ascari and Ferrari both drove their cars back to Milan and as they approached a level crossing Ferrari, who was following Ascari, braked a bit too late, and hit the rear of the latter's Alfa. Ascari was not pleased and the future commendatore had egg all over his face! ■

• **11**_ November 1920: an advertisement for the Ascari garage exploits the result of the flying kilometre at Gallarate. *(Alfa Romeo archives)*

Chapter 3
1920-1923
Red cars and
black shirts

taly was in a state of extreme upheaval during the 1920-21 winter. At the very moment of the Gallarate flying kilometre the political situation in the country was very serious. On 12th November Italy signed the Rapallo treaty renouncing Dalmatia and recognizing the independence of Fiume. D'Annunzio rebelled against this and declared war! The government sent in the army to re-establish order and a few canon shots were enough to force the seditious writer to abandon the siege and go home. But despite its pathetic ending his expedition had reawakened the most demagogic form of nationalism and contributed to fanning the flames of fascism. In January 1921, a split emerged at the Socialist party's congress in Livorno between reformists and revolutionaries. It led to the formation of the communist party - as would soon happen in France at the Tours Convention - inspired by the writings of Antonio Gramsci, a theorist of the workers' movement, who advocated a people's revolution on the model of the new Soviet Republic.

On 23rd May the reopening of the big store "Le Rinascite" set all Milan buzzing. It was a popular, star-studded event as the shop had been burned down in 1918 but was now bigger, better, more beautiful and more modern than before. The townspeople were given a day off to celebrate the occasion. The store was surrounded by shows and concerts including the Darclée Company, which put on a Franz Lehar operetta in the Diana theatre. At 23h00 a bomb exploded killing seventeen people and injuring many more. Terrorists under the anarchist banner claimed responsibility for the attack. Two young people were arrested but not the third who had set off the explosion. The circumstances surrounding the

affair have never been fully elucidated but the fascist party used the sense of outrage created by the carnage to rally a part of the electorate to their cause. The fascists, communists, socialists and anarchists among the Alfa Romeo workers began to show their true colours. However, in the competitions department the preparation of the cars for the coming season went on.

Alfa Romeo and racing have always been synonymous. It all began on 24th June 1910 when the company founded under the acronym A.L.F.A began production on the Portello site where it had bought the former Darracq factory. In 1911, A.L.F.A entered a works car for the first time in the Targa Florio, a Type 24 HP as well as a 15 HP model in the Modena endurance race. The factory's first win came in 1913 (a double) in the Parma-Poggio di Berceto hill climb won by Franchini from Campari. A 4.5 litres Grand Prix car was built in 1914 but was not ready for the Lyon event and then the war put a stop to everything. In September 1915, financial problems led to the liquidation of the A.L.F.A Company and on 2nd December it was bought by an engineering firm directed by Nicola Romeo. The make was renamed Alfa Romeo and the factory became heavily involved in the war effort making military equipment like lorries, plane engines, etc.. Car production did not restart until 1920. Giuseppe Merosi, a daring engineer, and former surveyor from FIAT, directed the design studio and recruited young talent among whom was Luigi Fusi, then aged fourteen! "Merosi told me to have a look through the archives to familiarise myself with the secrets of technical design," he later wrote in his memoirs. "You'll join the design studio when you're older," he was told. In fact, he was taken on after only three months.

• **12**_ Antonio Ascari, Alfa Romeo works driver. *(DR)*

Fusi was to publish a book on the company's models, which became the reference work. As the spring of 1921 approached Merosi and his team prepared three short-chassied (2.90 m wheelbase) 20-30 ES Sport spyders like the car raced by Ascari in Gallarate. The straight 4-cylinder side-valve 4250 cc engine (102 mm bore x 130 mm stroke) put out 67 bhp at 2800 rpm. It weighed 1200 kgs and had a top speed of 130 km/h. A total of 124 cars were produced over two years up to the end of 1922. Although it was a series production vehicle the cars entered by the factory benefited from a few tweaks. Besides, the team still had the 4.5 litres Grand Prix model and the 1913 overhead valve 6 litres 40-60 HP A.L.F.A which, after the war, became a twin carburettor version with an increased compression ratio giving it a top speed of 150 km/h.

In addition to Ascari the other Alfa team drivers for the 1921 season were Enzo Ferrari, Ugo Sivocci and Giuseppe Campari to whom was entrusted the big 40/60 while the others drove 20/30 sports models. Of the four Enzo Anselmo Ferrari was to become the most famous. He was born on 18th February 1898 near Modena in Emilio Romagna. However, because the region was snow-bound his father was unable to declare his birth until the following day. Mr. Ferrari had a forge that made metal beams and employed some fifteen to twenty people. He was quite well

off and bought one of the first cars seen in the region. One day in 1908 he took his son to a race in Bologna and Enzo saw the great drivers of the era like Felice Nazzaro and Vincenzo Lancia in action in their FIATs, Nazzaros, Italas, Scats, Ceiranos etc.. It was the start of a life-long passion and he swore that as soon as he came of age he too would be a racing driver. In his memoirs* he admitted that as an adolescent he had three dreams: to become an operatic tenor, a journalist or a racing driver. He quickly gave up the first as he had neither voice not ear but thanks to his skills he did the second for a while writing reports about football matches in the *"Gazzeta dello Sport"* and later on he edited a yearly magazine dealing with the Scuderia Ferrari. He did, however, manage to fulfil his third passion up to a certain point. He won a few races notably the Circuit of Savio in 1923, and above all the 1924 Coppa Acerbo on the Pescara track but he soon realised that he lacked the necessary skills and courage and would never become one of the greats although he established a reputation of being the best judge of talent in the history of the sport. His first protégé was Uvo Sivocci, a former cyclist, and experienced driver whom he met at CMN and later persuaded to join Alfa Romeo where he teamed up with Ascari and Campari who was born in 1892 in Fanfulla near Milan.

(1) - "Piloti, che gente" See bibliography at the end of the book.

This was the same year as Nuvolari and throughout his life Campari was considered "Milanese" by his friends as he spent his childhood in the Lombardy capital. As much as Sivocci was thin and elegant Campari was enormous: he was a huge eater, a lover of cooking for whom there was no greater pleasure than making huge plates of spaghetti at home for his guests. Enzo Ferrari said he sweated like a pig over his pasta and that he was covered in black hair like a monkey! Campari was also famous for his love of opera and operettas – a passion he shared with Ferrari. In fact, all his life he dreamed of becoming famous as an opera singer rather than a racing driver. Although much more gifted than his friend he did not have the same vocal skills as a professional and in addition, racing occupied all his time and energy. He was raised almost next-door to the Portello factories and remained faithful to the Lombardy make throughout his career. He was a tough but fair rival on the track and thanks to his strong physique a redoubtable finisher always ready to snatch a last-minute victory.

At the start Ascari owed his Alfa Romeo seat as much to his large Milan dealership and his numerous clients as to his intrinsic skills as a driver. Apart from his win in the Parma-Poggia di Berceto hill climb, he had not done much else to prove himself as his races in the Targa and Mugello had ended in accidents. During the 1921 season, though, his skill behind the wheel blossomed. The first event was the Parma-Poggio di Berceto hill climb on 8th May. The outright winner was Count Niccolini in his 4.5 litres FIAT who beat Ferrari's record with a time of 35m 39s and into second came Campari in his big 40/60 Alfa. Ascari and Sivocci in their 20/30 sports cars came first and second in the 4.5 litres category while Ferrari retired.

A week after this event the last democratic parliamentary elections were held in Italy as a nationalist coalition that included the fascists won. The socialists gained 123 seats and the fascists 35 out of 535. Mussolini, who won in Milan and Bologna, began to exercise constant pressure on the parliament. This was the context in which it was announced that Mercedes would be racing in the twelfth Targa Florio on 29th May. It was a case of welcoming the former enemy which would be challenging the big Italian teams from FIAT and Alfa Romeo. The Turin firm sent a pair of Grand Prix models for its works drivers Ferdinando Minoia and Pietro Bordino while Giulio Masetti brought along his private FIAT. Alfa turned up with five cars including two 40/60s for Ascari and Campari whose aim was outright victory. Sivocci and Ferrari drove a

• **14**_ The 1914 Alfa Romeo GP car that should have raced in that year's ACF Grand Prix with the engineer, Giuseppe Merosi, at the wheel. This was ten years before the P2. *(Alfa Romeo archives)*

Vettura da corsa A.L.F.A tipo Grand Prix 1914

couple of 20/30 Sports models and there was a spare on hand. In the Mercedes camp Max Sailer was at the wheel of a big 7.2 litres 6-cylinder 28/95. He was a 39-year-old engineer who had finished third in the 1914 Lyon Grand Prix. Victory went to Masetti followed by Sailer and then came Campari, Sivocci and Ferrari in their Alfa Romeos. Ascari retired. On the Mugello circuit on 24th July he was again forced to abandon as a badly fitted wheel bearing melted. Alfa Romeo scored a triple thanks to Campari, Ferrari and Sivocci. Enzo Ferrari recalled an anecdote typical of that era. The riding mechanic had to weight at least 60 kgs. Ascari's, a man named Sozzi, was particularly small and thin. Enzo saw him racing towards his starting position dripping sweat. The explanation was that at Ascari's request he had filled his pockets with lead to meet the weight! He also carried a big hammer like the one used to unblock the wheel nuts. Why then did he not put the hammer in the tool box? "To threaten any driver who would not let him past", was the answer.

At the beginning of August Ascari together with the rest of the Milan team entered for the Alpine Cup, a regularity rally with a set average speed of 48 km/h. It was run over a distance of 2306 kms and Alfa Romeo entered 4-seater sports cars each of which had to carry two passengers. It was an excellent opportunity for famous racing drivers to give journalists a ride on the roads of Northern Italy. Nonetheless, it was a demanding event as to respect the average speed over hundreds of kilometres on the roads of that era was no mean feat. Ascari covered the first stages in a cautious manner and then after a navigating error was obliged to speed up with the result that he went off in a downhill section while attempting to avoid a cart. Max Sailer, who was following in his Mercedes, saw the Alfa Romeo and its passengers disappear into a ravine! Their fall was broken ten metres further down. Ascari was trembling like a leaf but was unhurt as was his mechanic. His two passengers including a cameraman filming the event suffered slight injuries. Sailer stopped and helped by his passengers administered first aid. Then Ferrari and Sivocci did the same and brought the injured to the Madonna di Campiglio hospital.

In October 1921 Alfa Romeo launched its new weapon the 3 litres straight 6-cylinder SOHC RL Supersports designed by Merosi, in its showroom in Milan and then at the London Motor Show, The XIIIth Targa Florio was held on 2nd April 1922 and attracted a large number of foreign and Italian entries. Among the forty-eight cars were six Mercedes, 7.2 litres versions for Sailer and Werner and 4.5 litres models for Salzer and Lautenschlager, winner of the 1914 French Grand Prix, plus a couple of supercharged 1500 cc cars. Masetti, the 1921 victor in his FIAT, was at the wheel of a private 4.5 litres Mercedes. Two Wanderers completed the German contingent. From Austria came four Steyrs and five Austro Daimlers one of which was driven by Alfred Neubauer, the future Mercedes-Benz team manager. French hopes were pinned on a couple of Ballots and a Bugatti. Italy was represented by four Ceiranos, a Chiribiri, two Diattos, five FIATs and six Italas. Alfa Romeo entered seven cars for Ascari, Campari, Sivocci, Ferrari, Clerici, Tarabusi (in the RL sports model) and Mrs d'Avanzano, the best lady driver of the time of whom Enzo Ferrari was an ardent supporter! Campari had a racing version of the RL and the others were at the wheel of 20/30 ES sports cars. It was Ascari who had the idea of painting a good luck charm on the bodywork of his car in the form of a green 4-leaf clover which would become famous on the racing Alfas. Masetti won the race from the Ballots driven by Goux and Forestier while Ascari came home fourth overall and first in his category. However, on the Mugello circuit the Alfas were routed as all four crashed. On 3rd September 1922 the Monza 'autodromo' just outside Milan was inaugurated. On 10th September the Italian Grand Prix was held on the newly-built circuit over a distance of 800 kms! Unlike FIAT Alfa Romeo had no car complying with the Grand Prix Formula regs and did not take part. Winner of the race was Pietro Bordino in his 8-cylinder FIAT at an average speed of 148.938 km/h from his team-mate, veteran Felice Nazzaro. The nearby presence of the new circuit galvanised the efforts of Portello and on 22nd October for the last of the Monza inaugural races Alfa Romeo entered cars for Ascari, Sivocci and Campari. The race was won by Frenchman, André Dubonnet, in his Hispano-Suiza.

The Italians had other things to worry about as the week after the race the fascists began their march on Rome. Using physical violence and provocation they took power by intimidating the politicians. A lot of blood was spilt and historians reckon that around three thousand of their opponents were killed as well as three hundred in their own ranks. The carnage came to an end on 29th October 1922 when Mussolini took the night train from Milan to Rome and the following morning he obtained the office of president from King Victor-Emmanuel III. On 16th November he presented his government and was granted full power becoming the youngest-ever Italian prime minister at the age of thirty-nine.

During the 1922-23 winter engineers Giuseppe Merosi and Giorgio Rimini, who directed the Alfa Romeo competitions department, decided to beef up their usual team and enter Grand Prix racing. They developed a special model to be driven by Ascari, Campari, Sivocci, Ferrari and a newcomer, Giulio Masetti. They were joined occasionally by Maria Antonietta d'Avanzo. The programme began with the Targa Florio on 15th April 1923. Alfa entered five cars, three 3-litres RLs for Ascari, Campari and Masetti and two RLs bored out to 3154 ccs to make them eligible for the 4500 cc class in the hands of Ferrari and Sivocci. No Mercedes were entered and the main challenge looked like coming from Boillot's Peugeot, Rutzler and Brilli-Perri's Steyrs and future constructor Alfredo Maserati's Diatto. Ferrari set off like a scalded cat and had an enormous accident on the first lap. Ascari, on the other hand, made a cautious start and by lap 3 taking advantage of retirements found himself in third place behind Rutzler and Maserati and ahead of his team-mate Sivocci.
In the fourth and final lap both Rutzler and Maserati retired and Ascari went into a comfortable lead followed by Sivocci. Alas, Lady Luck played a cruel trick on Antonio. Some two hundred metres from the finish (the race distance was 432 kms) his engine blew and all he could do was watch helplessly as Sivocci blasted past to take the chequered flag. He finished the race with a load of passengers on board who had jumped into his car when his mechanic disappeared just as he had managed to restart. Even so the Alfa Romeo double was confirmed.

Finally on 6th May he got that elusive win by taking the chequered flag in the race on the Crémoni circuit in a 3.15 litres Alfa with a streamlined rear which was timed at 157 km/h on the straight. Into second came Alfieri Maserati in his Diatto. Ferrari, who had just got married on 28th April in Turin, attended this race with his young wife Laura in the guise of a honeymoon! On 10th June Ascari and Masetti finished second and third overall behind Brilli-Perri's Steyr at

Mugello. Then Enzo Ferrari in an RLTF scored an important victory on the Savio circuit near his home in Emilia-Romagna. After this race the parents of the pilot Francesco Baracca, killed in combat in 1918, gave the driver and future constructor the emblem of their son's aircraft, a black prancing horse, as a good luck token. This horse also appeared on the shields of the town of Modena on a yellow background. After a slight redesign it became the most famous badge in the history of the motorcar, first of all on the Scuderia Ferrari Alfa Romeos in the 30s, and from 1947 onwards on all the cars made by the Maranello firm. On the morning of the event there was a race for motorbikes and Ferrari was very impressed by the daring performance of a young 21-year-old named Tazio Nuvolari riding an Indian: it was a pointer of things to come.

In the meantime Giorgio Rimini spurred on by FIAT's entry for the A.C.F race on the Tours circuit, decided to enter Alfa Romeos in an international Grand Prix. Why not the Italian one especially as it was to be the first ever European Grand Prix. FIAT, Benz from Germany, the American Millers and Rolland-Pilain and Voisin from France had all decided to compete in the event. At a dinner in a restaurant near Portello during the summer Rimini asked Ferrari, who, thanks to his contacts in the racing world, was already laying the foundations of his future career as the Milan firm's team manager, to find the best technical people available. Immediately

Enzo persuaded the top class FIAT engineer, Luigi Bazzi (also of Modena origins) to join Alfa Romeo. This was made all the easier by the fact that Bazzi had had a major spat with the FIAT management during the A.C.F Grand Prix. He joined Merosi's squad straight away and supervised the development of the GPR (Gran Premio Romeo, often called the P1) that was undergoing testing. It was a real racing car powered by a 1990 cc 6-cylinder engine with a bore and stroke of 65 x 100 mm, twin ignition (2 magnetos and 12 plugs). In normally aspirated trim it put out 80 bhp and had a top speed of 180 km/h. However, Alfa Romeo produced a supercharged version for the first time which upped the power to 118 bhp at 5000 rpm and top speed exceeded 200 km/h. This made it a very competitive package well capable of taking on the FIATs, Millers etc on the Monza circuit. Ascari, Sivocci, Ferrari and Campari spent most of August testing it on the "Autodromo." Antonio was timed at over 180 km/h on several occasions on the straight and confidence reigned in the Alfa Romeo camp. On 27th August two FIAT drivers testing on the newly resurfaced tarred roads went off one after the other. Giaconne died and Bordino got away with fractures and one hell of a fright! He then raced in the Italian and European Grand Prix with his arm in plaster! Another fatal accident occurred during official practice on 8th September. Ugo Sivocci left the track at the end of the straight, hit a tree and was killed instantly.

His mechanic was unhurt and when helpers arrived they found him weeping beside the lifeless body of the driver. The team was grief-stricken and as a sign of respect withdrew its cars. Carlo Salamano won the Grand Prix in his FIAT in front of over 200,000 spectators with Felice Nazzaro coming home second. After leading right from the start, Pietro Bordino retired on lap 41 in extreme pain as he was driving with only one arm.

Meanwhile behind the scenes Enzo Ferrari was doing his best to poach FIAT's top racing engineer, Vittorio Jano. Together with Vincenzo Bertarione who had gone to Sunbeam a year earlier he was the man behind the 8-clyinder supercharged FIAT 805s. Jano was a friend of Luigi Bazzi's who advised Ferrari how to go about winning the engineer's confidence. Enzo as was his wont probably talked up the story of how he convinced the Piedmontais to accept his mouth-watering offer on their first meeting (and come to live in Milan) even if Alfa was FIAT's sworn enemy. Furthermore, Ferrari and Bazzi persuaded several of Jano's collaborators to follow their boss, which helped prompt FIAT's decision to quit racing. Vittorio took up his job as chief engineer of the racing department, got down to work and within a few weeks the P2 was on the drawing board. One of the greatest cars in the history of Grand Prix racing saw the light of day during the winter and gave Alfa Romeo and its drivers undreamed of success.

The P2 was a two-seater complying with the Grand Prix regulations: 2 litres maximum with or without supercharger, a minimum weight of 650 kgs and a minimum cockpit width of 80 cms plus a riding mechanic. It was powered by a straight 8 1987 cc engine (bore and stroke 61 x 85 mm) with DOHC distribution and a Roots supercharger like the one already fitted to the Sunbeams and FIATs. It put out 140 bhp at 6500 rpm and had a top speed of 225 km/h. These figures show that technically speaking it was the yardstick for the era beating Sunbeam, FIAT, Bugatti and Delage despite the latter's extraordinary 2LCV 12 cylinder engine that had made its debut in Tours in 1923.

While awaiting the debut of the P2, Alfa Romeo entered its RLTFs in the Targa Florio and the Coppa Florio on 27th April 1924. The two events were run together, the first over its usual four laps and the second over five. Once again Ascari's race was cut short. He made a bad start and then driving pedal to metal passed all his rivals including Boillot's Peugeot only to be overtaken by Werner's Mercedes after a refuelling stop. In trying to catch the German he crashed, luckily without injury. Some spectators helped him to get his Alfa back on the road but he was disqualified for receiving outside assistance. Werner went on to win both the Targa and the Coppa followed by Masetti and Campari. To say that Ascari was furious would be something of an understatement! ■

• **17**_ Monza 9th September 1923: FIAT scored a double in the Italian and European Grand Prix on the new Monza circuit just outside Milan thanks to Carlo Salamano (1st) and Felice Nazzaro, who were at the wheel of the 8-cylinder supercharged Type 805 FIATs designed by Vittorio Jano. Pietro Bordino (seen here passing Willi Walb's Benz Tropfen) led the race for a long time in n°.2.

Chapter 4
1924-1925
Triumph
and tragedy

• **19_** Lyon 3ʳᵈ August 1924: Antonio Ascari with a little help from his mechanic sets off in the ACF Grand Prix that he led for several laps before retiring due to mechanical problems.

The first outing of the P2 was not in the 1924 A.C.F GP as is commonly thought. The car made its debut on 9ᵗʰ June on the Cremona circuit. Ferrari seemed to be the right choice to give it its first gallop as he had won the Savio event (setting the fastest lap) and a week later the Polesine race beating Nuvolari, having his first taste of 4-wheel racing in a Chiribiri, on both occasions. Finally, this honour went to Antonio Ascari who together with Campari had tested the first P2 that came out of the factory on 2ⁿᵈ June at Monza and in secret on the Parma Poggia di Berceto hill. Luigi Bazzi was the riding mechanic in the Cremona race run over 320 kms. The Alfa Romeo top brass plus Enzo Ferrari turned out in force for the car's maiden outing. Its bodywork had not been finalised and the engine developed only 134 bhp. Nonetheless, Ascari was timed at 195 km/h over a ten-kilometre section and he won the race easily averaging 152 km/h! Alfa then entered a P2 for the Coppa Acerbo on the Pescara circuit on 13ᵗʰ July to give the car a thorough shakedown before the A.C.F and

European Grand Prix. Campari was at the wheel but retired due to gearbox problems. Enzo Ferrari in a 3.6 litres RTL notched up his third consecutive victory ahead of Masetti's Mercedes. The Lyon Grand Prix was THE race of the season and Alfa Romeo sent along four cars for Ascari, Campari, Wagner and Ferrari. A few days before the race Enzo withdrew, officially because of ill-health. Was it a diplomatic illness? Whatever, his car did not race as no reserve driver was nominated. The three P2s were entrusted to Ascari-Ramponi in no.3, Campari-Marinoni no.10 and Wagner-Sozzi in no.16. Their main rivals were four FIATS (Nazzaro, Bordino, Pastore, Marchisio), three Delages (Albert Divo, René Thomas and a GP debutant Robert Benoist), three Sunbeams (Segrave, winner in Tours in 1923, Kennelm Lee Guinness and Dario Resta) and Count Zborowski's Miller in the role of outsider. There were also two Schmid SSs with sleeve valve engines plus the Type 35 Bugattis making their debut. They were an unknown quantity although Ettore was very confident about their chances.

When practice began their design set tongues wagging thanks to their Alpax knock off wheels, hollow front axles, lightness (680 kgs) and their immaculate turn-out. Five were entered for Chassagne, de Vizcaya, Costantini, Friderich and Garnier. However, their power output of 100 bhp and top speed of around 180 km/h seemed a little inadequate for the long straights of the 23.145 km circuit. In the race itself the Bugattis fell victim to an epidemic of punctures despite their knock-off wheels because of a wrong tyre choice. The team set up a huge tent in the paddock that contained sleeping quarters, toilets and kitchens a kind of forerunner of the modern-day motor home. That year there were only three Grands Prix on the Constructors' World Championship calendar (the ACF, Spain and Italy). The French race was a major event spread over a week as races for bicycles, motorbikes and cycle cars were held before the Grand Prix itself. On the Sunday over 200,000 spectators turned up many of whom had slept on the spot or in the sleeping compartments of special trains. In 1914, the A.C.F

Grand Prix was run over a 37-km circuit and the 1924 event (35 lap/810 kms) between Brignais and Givors some thirty kilometres south of Lyon used around two-thirds of the pre-war layout so ten years on it looked like being another historic race for the Lyon area.

Alfa Romeo dominated practice but the grid positions were drawn by lot. Cars were sent off at 30-second intervals in twos with the classification taking the gaps into account. The race started at 9 a.m as it was a long event and scorching heat was expected. The Sunbeams were unleashed before the P2s. Segrave led for the first two laps until he was overtaken by Bordino who had started from the back but by dint of an heroic effort fought his up through the field and took the lead from Campari, Lee Guinness and Ascari. The Bugattis had their first wheel changes, Segrave stopped to change plugs and Bordino ran out of brakes on lap 12. Ascari then went into the lead from Lee Guinness's Sunbeam, which had passed Campari. When the Italian came in to refuel the Englishman went into first place briefly

• **20**_ Same place, same date: Giuseppe Campari drove one of the other Alfa Romeo P2s to victory in the ACF Grand Prix.
(Henri Malartre museum archives)

until he too had to take on fuel. On lap 17 Campari led the dance from Divo's Delage but Ascari was in attack mode and passed both the Frenchman and the Italian on lap 19 making it an Alfa Romeo one-two. Then on lap 32 Antonio's car ground to a halt with defective plugs and overheating letting Campari into a lead he held to the chequered flag ahead of Divo and Benoist's Delages and Wagner's Alfa Romeo. First race, first victory for the P2!

In Turin the morning after the French Grand Prix, Giovanni Agnelli, the FIAT Boss was furious that Alfa Romeo had won thanks to Jano and a team of his company's former engineers. Both Italian makes withdrew from the San Sebastian Grand Prix on the Lasarte circuit on 27th September and victory went to Henry Segrave in his Sunbeam. Enzo Ferrari, who was to devote himself to his business dealings with Alfa Romeo for the next two years, attended the Italian Grand Prix at Monza on 19th October. The Portello company entered four P2s for Ascari, Campari, Wagner and Minoia. There were no Bugattis, Delages or Sunbeams and to cap it all FIAT withdrew the eagerly awaited 12 cylinder car on Agnelli's orders virtually putting an end to the Turin company's participation in Grand Prix

racing. Thus, the opposition to the Alfas at Monza was somewhat threadbare consisting as it did of two Chiribiris, four Mercedes and two Schmidts. This did not prevent over 200,000 spectators turning up for the Grand Prix. The starting grid was decided by drawing lots – a system that prevailed until the early 30s. Ascari took the lead on lap 1 and remained there until the chequered flag. He was followed home by Campari (relayed by Presenti as he was not feeling well) Minoia and Wagner giving the Portello firm a quadruple success. The race was particularly tough on the Mercedes drivers whose cars were exhausting to drive because of their rock-hard suspension. They also had to stop on several occasions to have plugs and drivers changed. Masetti and Neubauer were the best-placed but they were far too slow to match the pace of the four P2s. Minoia set a new lap record and then it was Ascari's turn to do the same with a lap in 3m 34.35s, a speed of 167.763 km/h. A fatal accident marred the race. On lap 44 of the 80 scheduled the Polish Count, Louis Zborowski, who had raced a Miller in Lyon and was now behind the wheel of a Mercedes, went off in the Lesmo curve and hit a tree. He suffered a fractured skull and died immediately. The Mercedes team withdrew its other three cars

• **21**_ Monza 19ᵗʰ October 1924: A delighted Antonio Ascari (centre) has just scored another victory in his P2 Alfa Romeo in the Italian Grand Prix. He is being congratulated by his team including riding mechanic Giulio Ramponi (on the left) and his bosses Nicola Romeo (moustache and cap) and Giorgio Rimini (hidden by Romeo) as well as his young son, Alberto (leather hat) in the arms of a friend.
(Maniago Collection)

Enzo Ferrari:
"A very daring driver"

"Antonio Ascari was an extremely daring driver who had a remarkable capacity for dealing with the unexpected. A kind of 'Garibaldi' as we said in our jargon! He was one of those daredevils who preferred courage and instinct to a meticulous study of the track whose corners they attempted to take quicker and quicker lap after lap pushing the car's grip to its limits. A significant episode comes to mind in this context. During the 1924 Italian Grand Prix on the Monza circuit the creator of the 'autodromo' and Clerk of the Course sent a note to the Alfa Romeo pit. 'If Ascari continues to take the "Cuvetta" in such a way that he endangers himself and others I'll have to stop him.' In fact, Ascari was coming out of the corner in increasingly wild slides as he was trying to take it faster and faster each time round. This friend of mine was killed at Monthléry the following year in his red Alfa Romeo when he was again showing his exceptional talent."
Extract from his book "Piloti, che gente."

as a mark of respect. Antonio deserved his win, which had been a long time coming, but it would have been all the sweeter had the opposition been up to scratch. He received a rapturous welcome from the Italian crowd. At the finish young Alberto dressed in a blue suit was lifted onto the tail of the P2 for a lap of honour with his father.

In 1925, Alfa Romeo concentrated on Grand Prix racing to the exclusion of the Targa Florio and other sports car events. It had the ultimate weapon in the P2 allied to a top-class driver line-up of Ascari, Campari and Gastone Brilli-Peri. There were no changes in the formula except that riding mechanics were banned. The first Belgian (and European) Grand Prix was on 28th June on the magnificent 14.914 km Spa-Francorchamps circuit which had already hosted a 24-Hours sports car race in 1924. There was a small field as neither Sunbeam nor Bugatti turned up and the only opposition to the three Alfas (Ascari, Campari and Brilli-Peri) came from four Delages in the hands of Divo, Benoist, Thomas and Torchy. Thus, there were only seven entries for a race lasting 805 kms! The Belgians were all for the French cars and drivers and showed considerable hostility to the Italians in their Alfa Romeos. Ascari took the lead in hot, sunny weather ahead of Campari and Divo. The Alfas were far too strong and the Delage drivers could do little about the Portello domination. On lap 2 Benoist went out with a punctured fuel tank and then it was Torchy's turn (ignition). René Thomas's car caught fire on lap 7 leaving only four cars in the race. As if that was not

• 23_ Monza 1925: Engineer Vittorio Jano stands in front of what many consider to be his master piece, the P2 Alfa Romeo.
(Alfa Romeo archives)

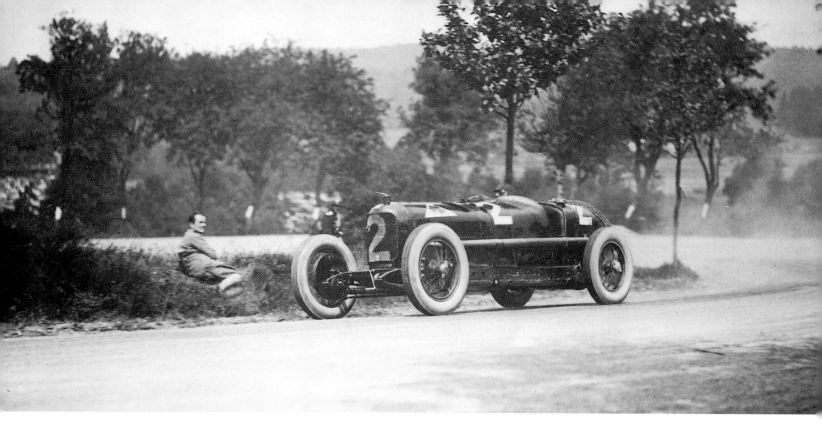

• 24_ Spa-Francorchamps
28th June 1925: Antonio Ascari
flat out in his P2 in the Belgian
Grand Prix in a part of circuit
which by-passed the Eau
Rouge corner. It was later
replaced by the Eau Rouge
Raidillon section.
(DR)

enough Brilli-Peri stopped on lap 28 with broken
suspension and five laps later Divo threw in the
towel with supercharger failure. And then there
were two! The race then took a surrealist turn.
Jano, who was infuriated by the anti-Italian
protests of the spectators, called in his two
drivers and served them lunch in their pits under
the boos and jeers of the crowd! Spaghetti for
Campari! After lunch they set off again to score a
rather inglorious double, but it was hardly their
fault, as they had no rivals. Ascari's talent
deserved better.

The A.C.F Grand Prix was held on 26th July
on the full Montlhéry circuit, inaugurated on
12th October 1924, which included the oval and
the road section (12.500 kms). The race was
scheduled for 80 laps, a total of 1000 kms. This
time there was stronger opposition to the three
Alfas as in addition to Delage (Benoist, Divo and
Wagner) Bugatti and Sunbeam entered. The
English cars in their traditional dark green were
driven by Segrave, Masetti and Conelli while the
Bugattis were entrusted to Costantini, Goux, the
de Vizcaya brothers and Foresti. Practice saw a
vicious dog-fight between the Alfa Romeo drivers
who were allowed free rein as their cars were
obviously quicker than their rivals. Given the
distance it was not the wisest of team policies.
The grid was again decided by drawing lots and
on the first row were P. De Vizcaya, Campari and
Segrave. The race started at 8 a.m. and the Alfas
immediately showed their superiority as Ascari
burst through from the second row to take the
lead at the end of lap 1 with eight seconds in
hand over Divo's Delage which was soon
overtaken by Campari. The French car's race came

• 25_ Spa Francorchamps
28th June 1925: Antonio Ascari
wins the Belgian Grand Prix
from team-mate Campari
giving Alfa Romeo a double in
the face of almost non-existent
opposition. Their success
received little applause from
the Belgian public.

to a premature halt when it stopped with supercharger problems. The two Italians pulled away from the rest of the field led by Wagner's Sunbeam, Brilli-Peri having been delayed by a plug change. Ascari came in to refuel and change his rear tyres on lap 15 and Campari took the lead. By lap 23 Ascari was back in front when for unexplained reasons he lost control of the P2 in the Couard dip. The wing nut on one of the front wheels became entangled in the wooden fencing which unbalanced the car and it overturned. Ascari was still inside when it finally came to a halt upside down. He died a few minutes later in the ambulance on the way to the hospital. Campari retook the lead but as soon as the Alfa Romeo team learned of Ascari's death they called in the remaining red cars as a sign of respect. The Benoist-Divo Delage scored a bitter victory. Antonio was only thirty-seven when he died and since then on the Montlhéry circuit there is a small memorial erected to the memory of the great Italian driver. The place of the accident was renamed the "Ascari curve." On 6th September Campari won the Italian Grand Prix on the Monza circuit from Diatto and Guyot in their Duesenbergs and thus gave Alfa Romeo the Constructors' World Championship title, which is a kind of legacy to Antonio Ascari's memory. ■

• **26**_ Linas-Montlhéry 26th July 1925: Antonio Ascari's last race. Here he rounds the "La Ferme' corner in his Alfa Romeo P2. He led until that fatal twenty-third lap. *(Alfa Romeo archives)*

Chapter 5
1925-1940
In the name
of the father

When Antonio Ascari was killed his son, Alberto, was a little boy aged seven years and thirteen days who was born in Milan on 13th July 1918. He grew up in the shadow of a father who was a champion racing driver at weekends in his Alfa Romeo and during the week managed a big garage that sold the Portello make's cars. Sometimes Alberto, his mother and sister came along of a Sunday to cheer on Antonio. One day during a practice session on the Monza circuit Antonio put his 6-year-old on son his knee, fired up the Italian Grand Prix winning P2 and set off on the circuit and once he was in fourth gear handed Alberto the steering wheel. However, he must have given him some help as to steer the Alfa required considerable physical strength. But one can imagine how proud of his dad the little boy felt! On 13th July the family had celebrated Alberto's seventh birthday and a few days later Antonio left the family house, near Lake Majeur, and set off for France to race in the A.C.F Grand Prix on the Montlhéry circuit. This time Alberto and his mother stayed at home. When and how did Elisa Ascari (maiden name Martinelli) learn the dreadful news? How did she break it to her son? Whatever the case on 30th July the day of the funeral the little boy walked to the cemetery with dignity his hand held by Giulio Ramponi, Antonio's mechanic. Giuseppe Campari embraced Alberto telling him that one day he would be more famous than his father.

• **27**_ Alberto Ascari with the latest 1939 500 cc Bianchi Corsa which he rode to several victories that year. The bike was derived from the famous sports "Freccia Azzura" and its 496.40 cc engine (bore and stroke 82 mm x 94 mm) put out 47 bhp at 6200 rpm. It weighed 195 kgs and was capable of reaching 195 km/h. *(Bianchi factory archives) DR*

"La signora" Ascari was a courageous and energetic woman. Fortunately she was well looked after in these tragic circumstances and given good advice by her own family, her late husband's and their friends from Alfa Romeo. In that era, the competitions department like that of most of the other constructors, owed its existence to the sales service because racing and winning helped sell the company's cars. It should be made clear that the saying "Racing improves the breed" had only a very relative application as while certain technical improvements undoubtedly arose from competition their application was fairly relative to say the least. The main reason was, of course, publicity. At the start of the 20s in addition to the FIATs and other makes which kept the cash coming in to the family garage, the 20/30 ES Sport, RL and RL/TF Alfa Romes came and went on a regular basis. Antonio was an excellent test driver and was always one of the first to try out the latest models or developments coming out of the nearby Portello factory either at Monza or on the local roads sometimes accompanied by a privileged client such as a racing driver or rich enthusiast. In April 1925, he tested the 6 C 1500, a little sports car with a SOHC engine designed by Vittorio Jano in keeping with his philosophy of transferring technical innovations from racing to road-going vehicles. The 6 C was to have a great future with a twin cam version in 1928 and then in 1929 the famous 6 C 1750 model.

Mrs Ascari did not have the same business acumen as her late husband. First of all, she concentrated on looking after the sales and accountancy side of the family business and delegated the maintenance of the cars to the workshop chief. Then little by little she handed over the reins of command to one of Antonio's brothers. The test and development aspect was reduced by circumstances as at the end of 1925 Alfa Romeo withdrew from racing for an indeterminate period after winning the Italian

Grand Prix and the Constructors' World title. Financially, the firm was in deep trouble. It was the just right moment to exploit race victories and make road-going cars. This began with the RL which was built up to 1927 as well as the 2-litres 4-cylinder RM launched in 1923 (produced up to 1925) and of course, the 6 C 1500. Furthermore, Alfa Romeo had gained a good reputation for aircraft engines and received orders that helped it to survive.

As a child Alberto was not the best of students. In secret and in memory of his father's exploits he dreamed of Alfa Romeo and races to come. He was nine when the first Mille Miglia was held in 1927: it was the start of a legend. The rostrum was monopolised by the OM drivers with victory going to one of his father's former team-mates, Ferdinando Minoia. Alfa Romeo did not enter as stated earlier but the Portello Company would have its revenge in the years to come. At home Alberto must have heard about the creation of the Scuderia Ferrari in Modena in 1929 managed by another of his father's former friends, Enzo Ferrari. Little did he know that this man would be his future employer! While he dreamed of racing he knew that he could not expect any encouragement from his mother who had already suffered one tragic loss and would not tolerate such an idea. He was thirteen in 1931 the year when Alfa Romeo launched its fabulous supercharged 8 C 2300 cc model in both racing and touring trim. The car was another of Jano's designs. Its racing debut was in the Mille Miglia in April and it was beaten by Caracciola's Mercedes-Benz SSKL. On 10th May it won the Targa Florio in the hands of Tazio Nuvolari, and two weeks later came first in the 10-hour Italian Grand Prix driven by Nuvolari-Campari. The two-seater was then called the Monza in honour of this victory. A client car won the Le Mans 24 Hours race thanks to British privateers Birkin and Howe. In parallel Alfa Romeo was developing the Tipo B single-seater, which became known as the

P3. It won its first Grand Prix, the A.C.F event on the Reims circuit in July 1932, driven by Nuvolari, the man from Mantua whose parents had bought grain from Antonio Ascari's! On 10th September 1933 the Monza Grand Prix run in two heats and a final was marked by three fatal accidents which claimed the lives of Borzacchini (Maserati), Campari (Alfa Romeo) in the second heat and that of Count Czaykowski whose Bugatti went off in the same spot in the final. It was a sad day for the Ascari family as Campari had been very close to Antonio. There was no way Alberto could mention his wish to race to his mother. However, a friend lent him a motor bike to do a few rounds of a square in Milan and in addition, he knew a couple of racing motor cyclists, Silvio Vailati and Nino Grieco. He had no doubts about what he wanted to do. He thought up a way of renting a

motorbike from time to time without his mother knowing. Only his sister was let in on the secret. When he was sixteen he could not hold back any longer and bought himself his own bike, a 500 cc 2-cylinder Sertum. Then followed a number of hard talks with his mother whom he called "il Maresciallo" (the marshal). The upshot was that during the week he left his bike at home while he continued his studies in a boarding school in Arezzo in Tuscany. He went on to study science in Macerata even further from his home. Soon, he quit from college as it bored him. In June 1936 just before his eighteenth birthday he entered for a regularity event in the north of Italy, the AC Milan 24 Hours. The event ended in a fall when he ran out of brakes but he made up for it a week later by winning his category in a trial on his repaired Sertum. In November 1936,

• **28_** Tazio Nuvolari at the height of his glory in one of the single-seater Scuderia Ferrari P3 Alfa Romeos. *(Ferrari factory archives)*

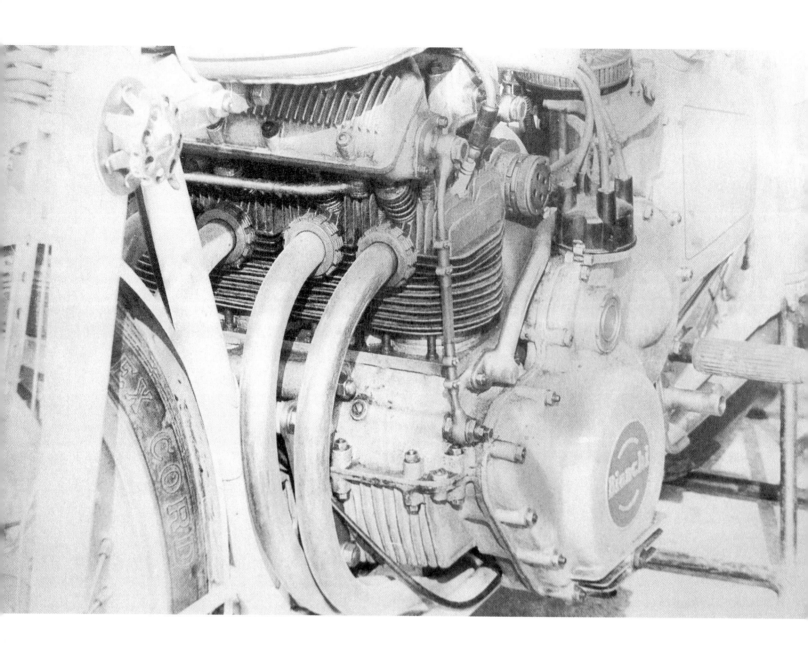

• **29_** The magnificent 4-cylinder supercharged 500 cc Bianchi engine with double overhead camshafts that Ascari tested on a motorway in early 1940. Then the war intervened and the bike never raced.
(Bianchi factory archives)

a group of amateur riders founded an independent team, the Scuderia Ambrosiana one of whom, Luigi Villoresi, was to become famous. He raced Maseratis and his brother Emilio made his debut in Alfa Romeos. The Scuderia Ambrosiana (like the Scuderia Ferrari) set up a motorcycle section running Gileras. It was this team that gave Alberto his break as in 1937 he did around ten races for the Scuderia winning five. He had passed his driving licence and had a Fiat Ballila. The Ascari garage had become a Fiat dealership and Alberto began to take an interest in its management.

In 1938, Bianchi offered him a works ride with a 300 lira per month salary plus prize money. The make founded by Edoardo Bianchi in Milan in 1885 enjoyed considerable prestige in the field of sports bicycles and motor bikes. The firm also built touring cars and lorries.

The two legendary Italian rivals of the 30s, Nuvolari and Varzi, had both won races riding Bianchis. Dorino Serafini had also made his name on the same bikes before being recruited by Piero Taruffi for Gilera in 1938 and both of them would drive works Ferraris after the war. Alberto accepted immediately and found himself with Guido Cerato and Aldo Rebuglio as teammates. In fact, a difficult task awaited them as the single-cylinder Bianchi seemed outdated in comparison with the multi-cylinder bikes of its rivals. The firm's budget was reduced as was the number of races due in part to petrol rationing in Italy at this period. Nonetheless, the three riders notched up a few good results. Alberto won the Circuit of Piacenza event run over one lap of the 54.130 km circuit in 45m 21s at 111,140 km/h from Cerato and scored another succes in the Cremona race (1h 8m 10s, 81,113 km/h). In 1939, he resigned for Bianchi and won the Siomma

Ligure races on 25th June and then in the Salzbourg 6-Day event in August. Out of thirteen starts for the firm he won five times, was on the rostrum twice and retired six times. He forged a reputation as a fighter. At the very beginning of 1940 when Italy was still hesitating about going to war he tested the new 4-cylinder 500 cc Bianchi with which the firm hoped to wallop BMW, AJS, Velocette, Guzzi and Gilera, at Monza and on the Milan-Turin Motor Way. Its engine put out 52 bhp at 7500 rpm and its top speed was in the region of 210 km/h. But war was looming and Bianchi decided to concentrate on bicycles and military vehicles. Although fighting had now been going on in Europe for over six months and the Germans were about to invade Belgium and France, the Mille Miglia was held on 28th April 1940 in an extremely tense international climate. Italy had signed the "Steel Pact" with Germany and adopted a neutral stance at the beginning of

the war. Thus, the race in which German and French teams took part was surrounded by a kind of Alice in Wonderland-like ambience. It was all the stranger as the event was held in 1939 after an accident the year before when a Lancia Aprilia had gone into the crowd killing seven children. The 1940 Mille Miglia (usually a single leg of 1600 kms) was called the Brescia Grand Prix and run over nine laps of a 165 km road circuit which included numerous straights passing by Cremona. No towns were crossed and thanks to this measure the organisers from Brescia hoped to be able to control the spectators and provide them with better protection.

This was the event in which Alberto Ascari made his 4-wheel debut. His car was a completely new open 2-seater called the "815." It had been designed and built in Modena by Auto Avio Costruzioni, the company set up by Enzo Ferrari after his departure from Alfa Romeo on

• **30**_ Milan April 1940: Alberto Ascari seen at the wheel of the brand new "815" open 2-seater which he raced in the Brescia Grand Prix. *(Ferrari factory archives)*

1st October 1939. The Portello company had paid
him compensation but in return he did not have
the right to build cars under his own name for
four years. He got round the problem by using
the above-mentioned name. He asked the
engineer, Alberto Massimino, helped by Vittorio
Bellentani and his friend Enrico Nardi to design a
sports car using FIAT parts. The engine was a
1496 cc straight 8 made up of two blocks laid
end to end with a special crankshaft and
distribution system. "Superleggera" aluminium
bodywork by Touring clothed the chassis built in
Nardi's workshops. The latter was a wooden

steering wheel specialist and would be a long
term Ferrari supplier: he also built small sports
cars based on FIATs. Nardi was Rangoni's team-
mate in the other "815." The two cars were
hastily constructed at Touring in Milan not far
from Corso Sampione. The Marquis Lotario di
Machiavelli (a descendant of the author of 'The
Prince') had bought one of the cars and Ferrari
agreed to sell the second one to Ascari for
20,000 lira. Alberto was at the workshops nearly
every day to see how things was progressing and
his co-driver was his cousin, Giovanni Minozzi, a
nephew of the late Antonio Ascari.

• **31_** Tripoli 12ᵗʰ May 1940:
This Grand Prix for
"Voiturettes" was the last
pre-war race for the Italians.
The flag has just dropped and
Alberto Ascari in his 6 CM
Maserati n°.6 is slightly ahead
of Carlo Pintacuda's Alfa
Romeo 158.
(DR)

The special BMW 328s were favourites for the race and the German firm entered five cars, two coupes and three open-tops. The 6-cylinder BMW engine with its special hemispherical cylinderhead put out around 140 bhp and the streamlined coupes driven by Fritz Huschke von Hanstein (the future Porsche team manager) and Count Giovanni Lurani were capable of 210 km/h. The Watney Team entered a couple of 3 litres Delage D 6 for Chinetti-Taruffi and Comotti-Rosa and the works Alfa Romeo 6 C 2500s were entrusted to regulars like Pintacuda, Farina, Biondetti and Trossi. Their engines developed around 145 bhp but they were much heavier than the BMWs. So what could a young driver like Ascari in a car that had just come out of the workshop, hope to achieve against hardened professionals in tried and tested vehicles?
A win in the 1500 cc class perhaps if he made it to the finish. On 28ᵗʰ April the two "815s" left one after the other, Rangoni at 6h20 and Ascari at 6h21. He soon overtook Rangoni and went into the lead in the 1500 cc class. On lap 2 the distribution failed and he had to retire. The other car did not get much further and went out with mechanical failure.

In early 1940 Ascari wanted to try his hand at single-seaters and bought a drive in Piero Taruffi's 6 CM Maserati. The two men knew each other from their motorcycle days when Alberto had asked Taruffi to incorporate him into the Gilera team as its bikes were much quicker than his Bianchi. In vain as there were no rides available. Taruffi agreed to lend Alberto his Maserati for two races, the Tripoli GP and the Targa Florio, in return for 12,000 liras.
On 12ᵗʰ May he lined up on the grid for the Tripoli event having set the twelfth quickest time in practice and came home ninth, not bad for a beginner in an outdated car. The race was dominated by the works Alfa Romeo 158s driven by Farina, Biondetti and Trossi. Villoresi in his Maserati came home fourth some two minutes behind the winner. Exceptionally, the Targa Florio on 23ʳᵈ May in Palermo was held on the short circuit (5.700 kms in the "parc della Favoritta") and was open to single-seaters. Victory went to Villoresi from Franc Cortese while Ascari crashed and damaged the Maserati. On 26ᵗʰ May he rode in his last motorbike race in Genoa and on 10ᵗʰ June Italy went to war. ∎

Chapter 6
1940-1948
Master and disciple

• **32**_ 2ⁿᵈ October 1948: The first post-war British Grand Prix was held on the Silverstone circuit and the Scuderia Ambrosiana Maseratis scored a double with Villoresi (n°.18) winning. Here he is followed by Ascari in n°.11.
(Maniago collection)

Alberto Ascari tried to find an outlet for his driving talents during the war. He set up a small transport company with the help of one of his uncles and his friend Luigi Villoresi. Its job was to transport fuel and vehicles to North Africa which still held strategic importance for Italy. It also helped him to avoid conscription. However, he had to hide when the Germans invaded Italy and tried to enrol physically fit young men by force. He was able to survive thanks to the family business, which he reorganised while awaiting the return of peace. One day in 1940 Villoresi introduced him to a charming young blond, one of the Tavola sisters who were family friends. Maria Antonietta known as "Mietta" and Alberto fell in love and started living together. They were married in Milan on 22nd January 1942 and their son, Antonio (known as Tonino) was born on 2nd August. Alberto was now a young businessman and his wife hoped that he would never race again. In 1943, he sold his "815" for twice the price he had paid for it. While the Ascaris managed to avoid the worst ravages of the war they lived in a state of permanent anxiety. Salvation came when the Allies landed in Sicily. Mussolini was deposed and reconstruction of the whole country began thus clients were beating a path to Ascari's garage.

In 1946, Villoresi and his friends resuscitated the Scuderia Ambrosiana. Many racing cars that had remained hidden in barns and on farms in the country suddenly reappeared. Following the Grand Prix organised by the French in the Bois de Boulogne beside Paris in September 1945 the Italians decided to do the same. Grands Prix were organised in Nice, Marseilles, Pau, Angoulême, Perpignan, and Albi and in Italy San Remo, Pescara, Bari, Turin, Milan, Modena and Syracuse followed suit. Alberto was a father for the second time thanks to the arrival of a daughter called Patrizia and as can be seen in his photos had developed a bit of a paunch and a podgy face. He did not seem in any particular hurry to start driving again. But his passion was still intact. He accompanied Villoresi to races and finally in Naples he was unable to

contain himself any longer and got in behind the wheel of a 1500 cc 4 CL Maserati. Straight away without any practice he reeled off a number of very quick laps, which left his friends open-mouthed with amazement. At the end of the year he did some private testing with the same car on the Monza circuit. He probably kept it from his wife!

Then at the beginning of 1947 he was one of the drivers who received a tempting offer from Piero Dusio, the well-off constructor of the Cisitalias and himself a racer. He accepted an invitation to join the "Croisière Cisitalia," which was aimed at raising the profile of the fledgling make abroad. Twenty-two identical single-seater D46s based on Fiat 1100s were sent to Egypt for a series of three races in Cairo and Alexandria organised by King Farouk. Like Formula France in 2000 lots were drawn among the drivers for the cars. The first race in Cairo was run on a 1.5 km circuit in two 25-lap heats and a 50-lap final. Franco Cortese won the first heat and Piero Taruffi the second followed by Ascari. In the final Taruffi took the lead from Cortese and Dusio but then had to retire. Alberto drove an excellent race overtaking Dusio and finished second thirteen seconds behind the victorious Cortese.

The other events in Egypt were cancelled and back in Italy Ascari drove a Cisitalia in the "Circuito dei Termi de Caracalla" in which he retired. In July he raced in France for the first time on the Albi track finishing fifth. It was now time to get down to the nitty-gritty. A projected comeback with Bianchi fell through as the Milan company which had been heavily bombed during the war did not have the necessary funds. So he turned to the newly relaunched Scuderia Ambrosiana outfit. The team entered cars and looked after the logistics but each driver had to pay for his seat. Gigi Villoresi who was racing a 4 CL Maserati convinced Ascari to buy a car of the same make as the firm had just brought out its 4 CLT complying with the new Formula 1 regulations. Ferrari was in the process of setting up his factory and there was no sense in approaching Alfa Romeo as the Portello Company refused to sell its Alfettas to privateers,

• **34**_ Rome 25th May 1947:
A very rare shot of Ascari in a
Cisitalia D 46. His race on the
"Termi de Caracalla" circuit
ended in retirement.
(Maniago collection)

even if the person in question was the son of the great Antonio. Luigi Villoresi's dislike of the make was accentuated by the fact that his younger brother, Emilio, had been killed testing a rear-engined Alfa in 1939. So for him Maserati was the only answer. Indeed, he had become Ascari's mentor, a role he was no longer able to fulfil in relation to his deceased brother, advising him about racing cars and showing him the ropes on the track. A deep friendship grew between the two men. Alberto bought a 4 CLT for five million lira. He put up three million himself, borrowed part of the remainder from Villoresi and persuaded Maserati to give him credit. He also became a share holder in the Scuderia Ambrosiana.

The 4 CLT was a single-seater powered by a 1.5 litre 4-cylinder 16-valve square engine (78 x 78 mm bore and stroke) with two stage supercharging. It put out around 260 bhp at 7000 rpm, was lower and more powerful than the 4 CL and well able to match the 1.5 litre supercharged ERAs and 4.5 litres unsupercharged Talbots. Ascari's first race in it was the Reims

Grand Prix, a 51-lap event on the Reims-Gueux circuit on 6th July 1947, the total distance of which was 405 kms. Alberto was sixteenth fastest in practice while pole was set by Swiss, Christian Kautz in a 4 CL in 2m 51.1s. It was the Italian's first time in the car and on the circuit. The Maserati was completely unsorted and the result was a blown engine, which did not help his financial situation. On 20th July Alberto entered for the Nice Grand Prix held on the "Promenade des Anglais." The circuit consisted of two long parallel straights beside the sea. He was third fastest in practice and came home fourth behind Villoresi's winning Maserati, Wimille's Simca-Gordini (with whom he battled until slowed by gearbox problems) and Parnell's ERA. There were a lot of city circuit Grands Prix in this era and after Nice came the Alsatian event in Strasbourg on 3rd August. The Scuderia Ambrosiana 4 CLTs driven by Villoresi and Ascari faced tough opposition from other Maseratis including those entered by the Naphtra Course team for Frenchmen "Raph" and "Levegh," Henri Louveau's Scuderia Milano entry plus the Lago-

Talbots in the hands of Charles Pozzi, Yves Giraud-Cabantous and Louis Rosier, Jean-Pierre Wimille's Simca-Gordini and a brace of Delahaye 135 Ss for Eugène Chaboud and Pierre Meyrat. In practice Ascari was second quickest in 1m 48.8s, 3/10 slower than Villoresi and he had his first spell as leader of a race before retiring with a broken valve, victory going to Villoresi. On 10th August they took part in the Comminges Grand Prix in Saint-Gaudens. Villoresi was again quickest in practice followed by Ascari in a 4 CL. The race was run in pouring rain and Villoresi retired after colliding with "Raph." The conditions were ideal for the big Lago-Talbots, which scored a triple with Chiron winning from Giraud-Cabantous and Chaboud. Ascari could do no better than seventh.

He really made people sit up and take notice for the first time in the Italian Grand Prix on 7th September. As reconstruction work on the Monza circuit had not been finished the organisers were obliged to hold the Grand Prix, run over 345 kms, in the streets of La Fiera, a park in Milan. Alfa Romeo racing on home turf entered four 158s for Trossi, Varzi, Sanesi and Gaboardi which finished in that order trouncing the various Maseratis and Lago-Talbots that made up the rest of the field. Villoresi, driving a new 4 CLT, had to retire due to defective brakes. Ascari, though, hassled Sanesi for third place for a long time until he was obliged to stop to repair a fuel tank mounting point. He finally came home fifth having proved that he deserved a quicker car than the Maserati: an Alfa Romeo for example.

• **35_** A photo signed by Ascari seen here in the Scuderia Ambrosiana 4 CL Maserati before the Alsatian Grand Prix in Strasbourg on 3rd August 1947. He retired with a blown valve while victory went to his team-mate Luigi Villoresi in his 4 CLT. *(DR)*

The Portello firm did not race in the ACF Grand Prix on 21st September in the Lyon region. Among the entries were Ascari and Villoresi in their Maseratis and for Alberto the name Lyon must have brought back memories as it was there in 1924 that his father almost won the ACF Grand Prix in his P2 Alfa. This time victory went to a French car, a Lago-Talbot driven by Louis Chiron from Henri Louveau's Maserati. The Scuderia Ambrosiana cars both retired, Villoresi's with an engine problem on lap 4 and Ascari's on lap 63 (piston). They shared the fastest lap with "Raph's" Ecurie Naphtra Course 4 CL Maserati. Indeed, the battle between Ascari and "Raph" provided much of the excitement in the race until their cars gave up the ghost handing victory to the prudent Monegasque in his lumbering Talbot.

A week later Ascari was at the start of a sports car race in the streets of Modena at the wheel of an A6GCS Maserati. The lack of protection for spectators was to have tragic consequences. Giovanni Bracco lost control of his Delage trying to avoid another driver and went into the crowd causing several victims. The

race was black-flagged and the results decided in accordance with the regulations. Victory went to Ascari from Villoresi but he would certainly like to have scored his first win in less dramatic circumstances.

On 5th October there was a Grand Prix in Lausanne on the shores of Lake Leman in Switzerland over ninety laps of a 3.236 km circuit. Villoresi came home victorious from Jean-Pierre Wimille's Gordini. At the start of the race Ascari starting from pole gave them a good run for their money setting the fastest lap. On lap 28 his Maserati's brakes went on the blink as he came into a corner and despite putting the fear of God into himself managed to slow down using the gearbox and tyres by sliding the car. He avoided an accident by the skin of his teeth, drove slowly back to his pit and retired.

The final race on the 1947 Italian Championship calendar was in Turin. Frenchman Raymond Sommer won it easily in his works 2-litres V12 Ferrari 166 while Ascari retired hisA6GCS Maserati due to a broken gear shaft. He finished fifth in the Italian Championship

behind Villoresi, Varzi, Trossi and Sanesi who were all older than him. However, Ascari was the coming-man in Italian motor racing just as Ferrari represented the future as a constructor even if Maserati still had glorious days to come.

In 1948, Villoresi and Ascari spearheaded the Scuderia Ambrosiana attack and they eagerly awaited the new 4 CLT/48s, which were lighter than the previous version. Ascari sold his 4 CLT back to Maserati wiping out his debt while taking an option on the new car. Only Villoresi entered for the Nations Grand Prix on 2nd May and two weeks later they were both in Monaco for the revived round-the-houses race in old 4 CLs. Ascari set the sixth quickest time on his Monaco debut in 1m 55.9s, some 2.1/10s slower than pole man Farina in his 4 CLT. In the race itself he retired when in eighth place with a broken oil pump. Villoresi took advantage of his rivals' mishaps to manhandle his Maserati up to fifth way behind Farina in the lead. Then tiredness set in and Ascari took over bringing the car home in the same position. Farina won from Louis Chiron's Talbot, de Graffenried's Maserati and Maurice Trintignant's Simca-Gordini.

On 13th June a special F2 race was organised in Mantua, the birthplace of Tazio Nuvolari. He drove a Ferrari 166 in it and Ascari was at the wheel of a sports A6GCS Maserati with its wings and lights removed to make it eligible. Symbolically it was a kind of handing over of power as the great Nuvolari was now fifty-six while Ascari was not quite thirty. Tazio was obliged to retire after about ten laps due to exhaustion caused by his lung problems and Alberto finished in a modest fifth place as his car had virtually no brakes.

Finally Ascari and Villoresi got their hands on their new Maseratis for the San Remo Grand Prix on the tight Ospedaletti circuit on 27th June. They were fifteen kilos lighter than the first version. The race lasted over three hours and the Scuderia Ambrosiana 4 CLT/48s scored a double with Ascari leading home Villoresi. It was his first major victory and his popularity soared. The Italian Tifosi nicknamed him "Ciccio" (chunky) but his double chin and spare tyre belied his speed.

● 37_ Lyon-Parilly
21st September 1947: Alberto Ascari in the Scuderia Ambrosiana Maserati 4 CL about to pass Reg Parnell's E-type ERA during the ACF Grand Prix. Both drivers retired. The Italian went out on lap 63 after several stops to change plugs. Louis Chiron won the race in his Lago-Talbot.

On 4th July the Alfa Romeo works team made its reappearance with the 158s in the Swiss Grand Prix in Berne. Tragedy struck during practice when Achille Varzi overturned his Alfetta and was killed instantly. The Varzi family asked Alfa Romeo to take part in the race anyway. Three 158s started in the hands of Jean-Pierre Wimille, who was probably the best Grand Prix driver of the time, Felice Trossi and test driver Consalvo Sanesi. Wimille set pole in 2m 45.2s ahead of Farina 2m 54.3s and Villoresi in 2m 56.7s. Ascari started in fifth place with a lap in 3m 00.7s. On lap 2 Christian Kautz lost control of his Maserati and hit a bank. He was killed instantly and his was the third fatality of the weekend as in addition to Varzi, Omobono Tenni had met his death during the race for motorbikes. The 158s dominated the Grand Prix with Trossi emerging victorious from Wimille after the Alfa pits asked him to let the Italian win in homage to Varzi. Behind these two the Maseratis managed to worry the third works Alfetta, Farina first of all then Villoresi and Ascari. When Giuseppe retired Villoresi managed to slip into third ahead of Sanesi where he finished while Alberto saw the flag in fifth a lap behind the winner. It was not a bad result considering the fact that the 4 CLT/48s were giving away over 100 bhp to the Portello cars.

Ascari received his just rewards when Alfa Romeo called on him to replace Varzi for the ACF Grand Prix on the Reims circuit on 18th July. He drove the third Alfetta alongside Wimille and Sanesi. French colours were well represented with one Delahaye, two Simca-Gordinis (one driven by an Argentinian, Juan Manuel Fangio, making his European debut after being recommended to Gordini by Jean-Pierre Wimille) and no fewer than seven Lago-Talbots. The 4 CLT/48 (Villoresi) and 4 CLT Maseratis (Pagani, Sommer and De Graffenried) were not quick enough to challenge the Alfas especially on the long straights of the French circuit. Practice confirmed the 158s' supremacy as Wimille set pole in 2m 35.2s from Ascari (2m 44.7s) and Sanesi (2m 51.2s). On the second row was a pair of Lago-Talbots driven by Etancelin (2m 54.6s) and Chiron (2m 54.8s). Ascari was very happy with his second position of the grid as it showed the Alfa Romeo management that they could count on him especially as the 158 was far more powerful than anything he had driven up to then. Its supercharged straight 8 engine put out in the region of 360 bhp and its road holding and acceleration were far superior to the Maserati's. The one drawback was the car's very high fuel consumption, which required three

• **38**_ August 1948: Ascari scored his second victory of the season on the Pescara circuit in a Type A6GCS Maserati. Note the typical décor of the era!

• 39_ Turin 4ᵗʰ September 1948. The Italian Grand Prix was held in pouring rain on a circuit in the Valentino Park while awaiting the reopening of Monza. Ascari stops for a plug change after which he rejoined in twelfth spot. He clawed his way back up to a fourth place finish behind Villoresi's Maserati, Sommer's Ferrari and the winner, Wimille in his Alfetta.

(Maniago collection)

stops during the 500 kms Grand Prix. The race was another demonstration of Wimille's skills although Ascari stayed on his tail for a long time. Villoresi drove a brilliant race after starting from the back of the grid in his 4 CLT/48 Maserati. He passed Sanesi and got within striking distance of his young protégé when his ignition went on the blink forcing him to pit for a long time. This left the three Alfa Romeos in the first three places with Wimille leading from Ascari and Sanesi followed by the Talbots of Etancelin, Comotti and "Raph". On lap 36 the Frenchman came in to refuel and Ascari took

the lead, which he held until lap 40 when he too had to stop for a refill. And so the Alfettas scored a triple with Alberto finally finishing third as he was asked to let Sanesi past. Then came three Talbots and in seventh place Villoresi's Maserati which had been taken over by Tazio Nuvolari on what was his last Grand Prix appearance. Ascari and his fans including former driver and journalist Count Giovanni (Johnny) Lurani all thought that he would be incorporated into the Portello team. But this was not to be the case. In addition, Alfa's up-and-coming rival Ferrari was keeping a close eye on Alberto, who won the Pescara 4-Hour event for Sports Cars on 15th August in a works A6GCS Maserati (he took over Bracco's car after his own retired), which was enough to prompt Enzo to think about taking him on as a works driver for the 1949 season.

In the meantime the Scuderia Ambrosiana entered its two Maseratis for the Italian Grand Prix on the Park Valentino circuit in Turin on 5th September. They were driven by Ascari and Villoresi and their main opposition came from the three works Alfettas in the hands of Wimille, Trossi and Sanesi. However the talking point of this race was the debut of the new 1.5 litre V12 supercharged Ferrari 125, three of which were on hand for Nino Farina, Raymond Sommer and Prince Bira. The French driver proved to be the quickest of the trio and in a race run in pouring rain he gave the Alfas a run for their money as did Villoresi and Ascari. Victory went to Wimille thanks to a blinding display of wet-weather driving with Villoresi finishing second from Sommer and Ascari who drove the whole race without either visor or goggles. Both Trossi and Sanesi retired.

Next on the calendar was the first post-war British Grand Prix on the Silverstone circuit on 2nd October. Neither Alfa Romeo nor Ferrari sent cars which diminished the interest in the race from a sporting point of view. Their decision was probably motivated by financial considerations. Maseratis and Talbots there were in plenty. Villoresi and Ascari arrived too late for practice but in compliance with the regulations they were allowed to start from the back of the grid. They soon fought their way up through the field. By lap 2 they had already passed most of their rivals and were zeroing in on Bira's Maserati in third place behind Chiron and Etancelin's Talbots. On lap 3 Villoresi went into a lead he was never to lose, followed by Ascari. Thanks to quicker refuelling Luigi drew away from his team-mate (who had had his rear tyres changed) and won the race by fourteen seconds from Alberto lifting off as the finish approached. Into third came Bob Gerard's ERA.

After their mind-blowing display in England the Scuderia Ambrosiana drivers entered for the race on 17th October that heralded the reopening of the Monza circuit. Alfa Romeo could not give the event a miss as it was on their doorstep and neither could Ferrari as the circuit was only 100 kms from Modena. After his cars' promising debut in Turin he wanted to show Portello that he was a rival to be counted with and for him Monza was THE reference. The organisers received a top-class entry including four Alfettas (Sanesi, Taruffi, Wimille and Trossi), two Ferrari 125s (Farina, Sommer) three 4 CLT/48 Maseratis (Villoresi, Ascari and Bucci), five 4 CLTs (Ashmore, Brooke, de Graffenried, Pagani, Parnell), five Talbots (Chaboud, Chiron, Comotti, Giraud-Cabantous and "Levegh") and Harrison's ERA. Before the race Nuvolari, who was the guest of honour, came into the pits to say hello to Ascari whom he saw as his worthy successor, a gesture that could not have failed to inspire Alberto. The cars lined up in five rows of four with the four Alfa Romeos on the front one pole going to Wimille in 1m 58.3s, the only driver to break the 2-minute barrier. Behind on row two came two Maseratis and the two Ferraris with Ascari setting the eighth fastest time in 2m 10.1s, 1/10s slower than Villoresi. After the start Sommer was the only driver who managed to get among the Alfettas but he retired on lap 7 with an attack of asthma! This brought Ascari into seventh place and after Villoresi went out on lap 48 followed by Farina on lap 53, both with transmission problems, he found himself in fifth behind the Alfas where he stayed until the chequered flag.

Fifteen days later Villoresi won the Penya Rhin Grand Prix on the Pedrables circuit (Barcelona) beating Farina and Bira's Ferraris. Again there were no Alfa Romeos. Luigi did the "grand slam" as he also set pole and fastest lap in the race. Ascari in the other Scuderia Ambrosiana 4 CLT/48 Maserati had a frustrating Sunday. He was fourth quickest in practice but retired with a broken supercharger on lap 1. He was not too disappointed as he knew that both Ferrari and Alfa Romeo were interested in him. ■

Chapter 7
1949
The men
from Maranello

• **40**_ Berne-Bremgarten
3rd July 1949: The start of the
Swiss Grand Prix. Ascari in the
n°.30 Ferrari 125 C is
alongside Bira's n°.22
Maserati and ahead of
Sommer's n°.18 Lago-Talbot.
He scored his first major win
in this event.
(Maniago collection)

January, chosen by General Péron and his acolytes to stage the *Temporada* from 1947 onwards, is one of the hottest months in Argentina. It consisted of a series of races held in Buenos Aires, Mar del Plata, Rosario and other towns in which temporary circuits were built. General Juan Domingo Péron was elected president on 26th February 1946 and governed the country with a shrewd mixture of authoritarianism and populism plus a dose of socialism and demagogy. Among the people Péron admired was the late Mussolini and like "il Duce" he was a lover of motor sport, and also knew the political kudos that could be gained from it. He organised lavish parties on the evening before and the day after the races in which Italian and French teams were invited to take part provided that they lent some of their cars to local hopes. In 1948, Juan Manuel Fangio had shown his talent at the wheel of Maseratis and Simca-Gordinis when racing against European specialists after which he had come to Europe where he made a relatively discreet debut in a Simca-Gordini. On 15th January 1949 Alberto Ascari flew to Buenos Aires along with his friend Luigi Villoresi. He drove the Scuderia Ambrosiana 4 CLT Maseratis, specially prepared by the factory, in the first two rounds of the Temporada. On 29th January a shadow was cast over practice for the Palermo Park event by Jean-Pierre Wimille's fatal accident. The great

French driver went off trying to avoid reckless spectators and was killed. This did not prevent the following day's race from taking place in an ambience of popular frenzy that combined chauvinism and enthusiasm. Ascari made an excellent start and drew away from his pursuers including Fangio in his spanking new 4 CLT/48 Maserati brought by the Argentinian Automobile Club. Juan Manuel was delayed by tyre trouble and could do no better than fourth. At the finish Ascari got the scare of his life! He saw a crowd of delirious spectators coming for him and took to his heels convinced that they were after him because he had beaten Fangio. He took refuge in a parked car and after three-quarters of an hour he finally got out only to realise that the crowd wanted to carry him aloft in triumph!

In the second race the "Premio Wimille" on 6th February run in pouring rain Ascari was again in the lead when one of the exhaust pipes on his Maserati broke and he had to retire. Farina won the Rosario event on 13th February in his Ferrari and Ascari finished third. Finally, on 27th February in Mar del Plata he ran into mechanical problems that prevented him from defending his chances and victory went to Fangio, it being the latter's first major win in a single-seater. The pundits were now convinced that the two stars of the future would be Ascari and Fangio and the coming season would prove them right.

In the meantime Ascari and the other drivers made a detour by Brazil to race in a couple of events. On 20th March on the Interlagos track in the suburbs of Sao Paolo he came fourth. Then on the Gavea circuit (Rio de Janeiro) he had a big shunt. He was battling with Fangio for the lead when he swerved to avoid a local driver who had gone wide just as he was overtaking him. This forced him into a wall and he went off into a field and hit a tree. Ascari was thrown out of his car and landed on the ground alongside it inhaling the exhaust fumes, which knocked him out. He was rushed to hospital with three fractured ribs and a broken collarbone.

When he got back to Europe he was forced to miss the San Remo Grand Prix, which he had won the previous year. Victory went to Fangio who dominated all his rivals. In the spring of 1949 the Argentinian's talent flowered on European circuits and after San Remo he racked up a string of successes in Pau, Perpignan and Albi in a Maserati and then in Marseille in a Simca-Gordini. His San Remo win helped him to land a works drive with Alfa Romeo the following year as the Milan company did not race in 1949 due to the loss of three of its top drivers Varzi, Wimille and Trossi (who died of cancer in the spring of 1949). Commercial and financial factors also played a role in this decision.

Ascari and Villoresi were negotiating with Ferrari whose cars were starting to make a name for themselves. In 1947, Enzo Ferrari's first car (under his own name) had made its racing debut in Piacenza in the hands of Franco Cortese: it was designated the 125 S and was an open two-seater powered by a 1500 cc V12 engine. It then raced in Rome where it won and in the autumn Sommer scored a victory in Turin. In those years engineers came and went with bewildering rapidity at Maranello beginning with Gioachino Colombo. He was born in 1903. He had worked on the Alfetta in Modena in 1937 and at the end of 1945 he started designing the 125 S but the car was completed by Giuseppe Busso, another former Alfa Romeo engineer, who had become head of the Ferrari design office in June 1946. In October of the same year Aurelio Lampredi from the aeronautics industry joined the Scuderia. He stayed for a year and then went to Isotta-Fraschini which was attempting a comeback. Colombo (who had gone back to Alfa Romeo) was back in Maranello on 1st January 1948 to become consultant for the planning office. He then worked on the 125 F1, a supercharged 1500 cc car, which had its first race in Turin in September 1948. The event in question was the Italian Grand Prix and Sommer finished third splitting Ascari and Villoresi in their Maseratis while victory went to Wimille in his Alfa Romeo 158. Ferrari was really beginning to make an

• **42_** Zandvoort 31st July 1949: Ascari overtakes the Alta driven by Geoffrey Crossley on his way to second place in the second heat of the Dutch Grand Prix. Note that both drivers are wearing helmets, which was rare for that era. Imposed by the Dutch organisers, perhaps?

impact in sports car racing with the open 2-litres V12 166, which notched up wins in the Targa Florio and the Mille Miglia in the hands of Clemente Biondetti followed by the Paris 12 Hours with Luigi Chinetti at the wheel.

1949 looked like being a rosy year for the fledgling Maranello company eighteen kilometres from Milan as its workshops gradually increased their production capacity. In 1947, three cars were built and the next year the total rose to five. Several 166 MMs (Mille Miglia) and 166s (F2) were on order from drivers or private teams while in F1 a new version of the car designed by Colombo was about to be launched. The 1949 125C differed from the previous model by an increase in power and a reduction in weight (560 kgs). The Scuderia was managed by Federico Giberti even though it was Enzo Ferrari who took the decisions. Already the latter was showing his famous reluctance to attend races and it was Giberti who noticed Ascari's skills at San Remo and Pescara. Of course Enzo, who was a friend of Antonio's and had sold an 815 to Alberto in 1940, knew exactly whom he was dealing with.

Even so like the Alfa Romeo management he was not entirely convinced early on. It was not until Alberto began to beat the top drivers of the moment like Farina, Bonetto and Sommer (whom Ferrari listened to) that he began to take his dead friend's son seriously. Alberto too had decided to end his collaboration with Maserati, which had given him his break, and wanted to come to Maranello. In May it was done and dusted. Corrado Filippini, a journalist and friend of both parties negotiated on behalf of Ascari and his friend Villoresi and on 27th May they signed their contracts in Maranello as works drivers. They both had the same terms and conditions starting with a monthly salary of 100,000 lira plus 50% of the starting and prize money from Grands Prix and any other race in which the Scuderia decided to compete. It was the first time that Ferrari signed a yearly contract that included a basic salary as up to then the usual practice had been to share the bonuses while deciding where to race on an ad-hoc basis. In his first outing for the team Ascari justified the new policy by winning the

• **43**_ Another shot of the Dutch Grand Prix on 31st July 1949 with Ascari in the lead at the start of the final from Villoresi. On lap 34 he lost a wheel and with it all chances of victory. He would have to wait till 1952 to win the Dutch event.

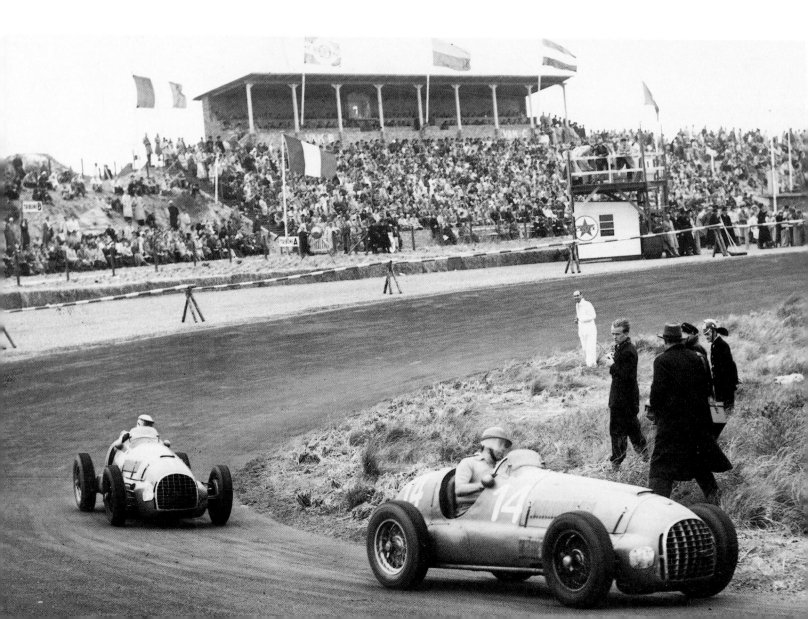

● **44**_ Silverstone 20ᵗʰ August 1949: Ascari in his 125 C Ferrari won the International Trophy run in two heats and a final. He dominated his rivals beating Farina's Maserati, Villoresi's Ferrari and De Graffenried's Maserati. He also set the fastest lap in 1m 56.4s, a speed of 149.234 km/h.

Bari F2 event. A week later Ascari and Villoresi made their F1 Grand Prix debut for the Prancing Horse in the Belgian Grand Prix. The very rapid Spa-Francorchamps circuit consisted of long straights and sweeping curves. The cars' rear suspension was modified with transversal springs replacing the torsion bars. In addition, Ascari who liked to exit corners at higher engine revs than the majority of his rivals wanted a shorter top gear installed, 3.27:1 as against 3.00 for Villoresi. This increased his fuel consumption slightly – the supercharged Ferraris were already much thirstier than the big unsupercharged 4.5 litres Lago-Talbots. In practice Villoresi was quickest ahead of Fangio's 4 CLT Maserati and Etancelin's Lago-Talbot while Ascari was back on the third row. At flagfall Villoresi took the lead from Farina's Maserati and Ascari who had made a blindingly quick getaway. Fangio soon retired as his car's engine was fit for the scrap heap and then Farina went off after setting the fastest lap. Thus the two Ferraris looked like scoring a run away victory with Villoresi leading Ascari. But the Italian cars were obliged to stop for fuel twice in the 507 km race as against once for the Talbots, which enabled Frenchman Louis Rosier to overtake them and win. Villoresi and Ascari finished second and third. It

was not a bad result but gave Ferrari and his young engineer, Aurelio Lampredi (born in Livorno in 1917) food for thought. The latter was Gioacchino Colombo's assistant, the man responsible for the early V12s from Maranello. In October 1949 he left Ferrari again for Alfa Romeo, which was getting the Alfettas ready for a return to the Grand Prix scene in 1950. Thus, Ferrari promoted Lampredi to the position of project leader for engines and racing.

The weekend after Spa was a full one for motor sport with the first post-war Le Mans 24 Hours race and the Autodromo Grand Prix at Monza. It was a very prestigious F2 race and Ferrari entered two 166 Cs for Ascari and Villoresi backed up by Bonetto's private 166 C and a couple of 166 Cs from the Argentinian Automobile Club for Fangio and Campos. Ferrari had asked the Argentineans for 11,000 dollars which was collected at the last minute and took a long time to reach Maranello so finally only one of the cars arrived at Monza on Friday. It was entrusted to Fangio who had tested it the day before and discovered that fifth gear was not working. Luckily for him both works Ferrari drivers ran into trouble: oil pressure problems hit Villoresi and Ascari was slowed by a recalcitrant gearbox after leading for

part of the race. Victory went to Fangio who
revved his Ferrari up to 7500 rmp in fourth on
the straights (500 rpm over the maximum) and
Bonetto and Ascari completed the rostrum
giving Ferrari a triple but not in the order the
Commendatore had expected. The same day
Luigi Chinetti won the Le Mans 24 Hour race in
his 166 MM *Barchetta*, the first of nine Ferrari
victories in the Sarthe.

The next F1 Grand Prix was the Swiss
event on the Berne circuit on 3ʳᵈ July. The 125 Cs
had been reworked by Colombo with input from
Lampredi. They were ready at the last moment
and did not reach the circuit until Friday evening
so the drivers missed the first practice session.
Ascari managed to put his car on the front row
with a lap in 2m 54.7s but was headed by Farina
and Bira in their Maseratis who lapped in
2m 50.4s and 2m 53.2s respectively. Villoresi was
back on the fourth row. He started with a full
tank and hoped to go the complete distance
without stopping. Ascari had forty-five litres less
at the start and his aim was open up a good
lead and then refuel. He hit the front
immediately followed by Bira while Villoresi
pushed his way up to third. Farina then began to
push, passed the Italian and the Siamese and
pulled in Ascari but his engine gave up the
ghost at quarter distance. Alberto's next rival
was Raymond Sommer's Talbot who was hoping

to repeat Rosier's Spa exploit. However, the
Ferraris had such a power advantage that even
refuelling once they were able to out-distance
their pursuers. Ascari won from Villoresi giving
the Scuderia its first win in an F1 Grand Prix.
Although the Formula 1 championship would
not be inaugurated until the following year it
was a noteworthy success.

Fifteen days later in the "Coupe des Petites
Cylindres" an F2 race on the Reims circuit Ascari
in his works 166 was again up against Fangio's
166 entered by the Argentinian Automobile Club.
This time Juan Manuel retired due to a broken
gear lever and Alberto went on to score an easy
victory. For reasons best known to himself Ferrari
entered only a single 125 C for Villoresi for the
French Grand Prix on 17ᵗʰ July. He made a good
start and was scrapping with Fangio's 4 CLT
Maserati for the lead until his brakes went on
lap 4. Veteran Louis Chiron won in his Lago-
Talbot from Bira's Maserati and Peter
Whitehead's private Ferrari which led until the
second last lap when he lost the use of fourth
gear. A rather grumpy Ascari was a reluctant
spectator!

On 31ˢᵗ July the Scuderia turned up in
Holland for the first Dutch Grand Prix with a
brace of 125 Cs. The Zandvoort circuit was
situated just beside the North Sea and
undulated its way through the dunes. What

Enzo Ferrari:
"He had to hit the front straight away"

In his first Memoirs "My Terrible Joys" published in Italy in 1963 Ferrari described Ascari as follows:
"Alberto Ascari was an outstanding driver and human being. He had unshakeable will power, knew what he wanted and was meticulous in every aspect of his job. He had a precise determined driving style but he had to start in front. Once he did this he was difficult to overtake. Indeed, I would go so far as to say it was impossible unless of course a fratricidal battle upset his judgement, as was the case at Monza in 1953. If he was in second place or further back he did not have the fighting spirit that I expected to see on certain occasions. It was not that he gave up but when he had to pursue a rival and overtake him he suffered not from an inferiority complex but a kind of nervousness that prevented him from expressing all his talent. He was the opposite of all the others. Generally speaking, the driver who is in the lead is worried about holding on to it. He cannot control what is happening behind him. He sets his pace and is not always sure he can maintain it. Alberto, on the other hand, felt completely at ease in the role of the hare which really brought out the best in him and he was unmatchable."

made it tricky was the wind, which tended to gust and blow sand onto the track. The race was run in two heats and a final. Villoresi won his easily but Ascari's was held in pouring rain and he finished second due to a damaged supercharger. This was changed by the mechanics and he was romping away with the final until six laps from the end when he lost a front wheel and ground to a halt. Victory went to Villoresi.

There was no doubting Ascari's speed but was he too hard on his cars especially when cornering, as the above incident would seem to suggest? On 20th August the two Scuderia drivers raced in a Formula 1 event in Great Britain the Daily Express Trophy on the Silverstone circuit also consisting of two heats and a final. Both came second in their heats Ascari behind Bira and Villoresi behind Farina. Were they sandbagging? Right from the start of the final a no-holds-barred battle began between Farina and Ascari with Villoresi in third (where he finished). Despite intense pressure from Farina's Maserati Alberto managed to hold onto a slender lead until the chequered flag setting the fastest lap in the process. A week later Farina had his revenge in the Lausanne Grand Prix after Ascari was slowed by brake problems. He finished second over a minute behind the Doctor.

Then came the Italian Grand Prix on the Monza circuit on 11th September. The spectator enclosures and grandstands were packed to overflowing by the *Tifosi*. Ferrari entered the latest version of the 125 C which put out 290 bhp thanks to an engine with four overhead camshafts and two stage supercharging. Ascari had tested the prototype at Monza a fortnight before the race and there were two cars on hand for himself and Villoresi. Sommer and Bonetto had the previous models and Whitehead entered his private 125. Opposition came from a horde of Maseratis the quickest of which were driven by Farina and Taruffi (Scuderia Milano) and de Graffenried and Bira. Completing the field were five Lago-Talbots in the hands of Rosier, Etancelin, "Levegh" among others plus Eugène Chaboud's Delahaye. In practice Ascari set pole in 2m 3s just 4/10s ahead of Villoresi. He drove a perfect race taking the lead at the start and opening up a gap lap after lap. Villoresi in second place was outdistanced and retired on lap 27. Alberto then came in for a plug change and was so far ahead that he rejoined without losing the lead. After Villoresi's disappearance Campos took up the chase until he too joined the dead car park leaving second place to Philippe Etancelin in his Talbot. And so Ascari ran out an easy winner with a lap in hand over the veteran Frenchman

• **47**_ Monza 11th September 1949: Alberto closed his very successful first season with Ferrari in the best possible manner by scoring a popular victory in the Italian Grand Prix as well as setting the fastest lap in 2m 06.8s, a speed of 178.864 km/h. Here he is about to pass Frenchman Guy Mairesse in his cumbersome Talbot.

after setting the fastest lap at around 178 km/h. It was a triumph for the Maranello constructor and Alberto who won the Italian Drivers' Championship from Villoresi and Farina. 1950 would see the first F1 World Championship for Drivers and Ascari was among the favourites.

However, the 1949 season was not over yet and in November he set off from Genoa for Argentina by boat for the Temporada beginning in mid-December. Travelling with him were Villoresi and Dorino Serafini, the former motor cycling champion, whom Ascari had succeeded at Bianchi in 1938 after Serafini had joined Gilera managed by Piero Taruffi. The first round was held in the Palermo Park in Buenos Aires on 18th December. It was a Formula Libre race called the "Premio Juan Domingo Peron" and Ascari won it in a supercharged Ferrari 166 from Fangio in another Ferrari. It is worth noting that the works Prancing Horse cars were sponsored by the drinks company Fernet Branca. The Ferrari delegation spent Christmas in Buenos Aires and on 8th January 1950 another race, the Eva Peron

Cup, was held in the Palermo Park. This time Ascari messed up his start and victory went to Villoresi with Fangio finishing fourth. Then in the Mar del Plata F. Libre event Ascari won again after Fangio and Villoresi eliminated each other in a risky overtaking manoeuvre. The final round in Rosario went to Villoresi while Ascari retired with cooling problems caused by a newspaper wrapped itself round his radiator. The partisan Argentinian press spilt a lot of ink during this Temporada trying to whip up public opinion against the Italians who had the audacity to beat the locals led by Fangio. This poisonous press campaign did not affect the drivers who held each other in mutual respect. The Italian team then spent a few days' holidays in Brazil before returning home. On landing in Rome they were congratulated by the young and future president of the parliament, Giulio Andreotti, before being given an audience with Pope Pius XII. Like in the Fascist past, Italian democracy and Vatican diplomacy were not averse to showing their support for racing drivers. ∎

• **48**_ Buenos Aires
18th December 1949: Ascari
wins again on the Palermo
Park circuit in a 166 F2
supercharged Ferrari. The
Trofeo Peron was run to
Formula Libre regulations, as
was the next event in the
Temporada in January 1950.
(Maniago collection)

49_ Geneva 30th July 1950: Although not counting towards the F1 World Championship the Grand Prix des Nations was another round in the Ferrari-Alfa Romeo duel. Ascari in his n°.40 Ferrari 340 F1 finished fourth behind the three Alfa Romeo 158s driven by Fangio (n°.4) de Graffenried (n°.6) and Taruffi (n°.46). Villoresi in the n°.42 Ferrari driven by Ascari in Belgium and Farina in the n°.4 Alfa Romeo were both eliminated by serious accidents. *(Maniago collection)*

Chapter 8
1950
Ferrari goes head to head with Alfa Romeo

The 1950 season saw a major innovation in motor racing as the FIA inaugurated the first ever Formula 1 World Championship. It consisted of six Grands Prix and points were awarded as follows: 8 for the winner, 6 for second and then 4, 3 and 2 down to fifth place and 1 point for fastest lap. In case of driver changes during a race the points would be shared. At the end of the season the best four results would be taken into account for the attribution of the title. The races were open to cars complying with the F1 rules, namely, 4.5 litres unsupercharged and 1.5 litres supercharged. There was no weight limit. Finally, to try and emphasise the world aspect the Indianapolis 500 Miles race was included although run to a completely different formula. Few were the Americans who came to race in F1 and even fewer were the F1 regulars who drove in the Brickyard. Indianapolis was finally taken off the F1 calendar for the 1961 season.

The main talking point as the championship got under way was the return of Alfa Romeo after a year's absence. The Milan Company had recruited three top-class drivers, Italian veterans Nino Farina and Luigi Fagioli plus Argentinian coming man Juan Manuel Fangio, the 3 Fs as they were called. In addition a fourth car was occasionally entered; for Reg Parnell in England and Toulo de Graffenried in Switzerland. Colombo, who had returned to Portello after his brief sojourn at Ferrari, had continued to develop the 158 which now put out 350 bhp at 8500 rpm. It was certainly the quickest car around (Fangio hit 310 km/h on the long Pescara straight) but was handicapped by excessive thirst.

Maranello confirmed Ascari and Villoresi plus Serafini recruited at the end of 1949 while Frenchman Raymond Sommer also drove in a few events. Aurelio Lampredi up-dated the 125 Cs but he was now working on a new car that would appear towards the end of the year. Together with Enzo Ferrari he saw that an unsupercharged car's power handicap was more than compensated for by lower fuel consumption. Thus, he designed a new unblown V12 exploiting the higher cubic capacity authorised by the regulations. However, Ferrari had to start the championship with the 125 C whose wheelbase had been increased to 238 cms and the rear track widened by 5 cms. From the Swiss Grand prix onwards it was fitted with a de Dion rear end. Power was increased to 315 bhp at 7500 rpm.

Opposition to these two came from the works 4 CLT/48 Maseratis of Franco Rol and Louis Chiron plus the Scuderia Milano entry for Felice Bonetto and the Ecurie Platé cars of Prince Bira, Toulo de Graffenried and occasionally Paris based American Harry Schell. The expected entries from Osca and BRM never materialised. The English cars suffered from a host of problems due to the complexity of their V16 engine while OSCA (the make founded in Bologna by the Maserati brothers after the Orsi family bought their company) was suffering from financial problems. The other makes that raced were French beginning with the Lago-Talbots. The T26 Cs were powered by a big 4493 cc long stroke straight 6 engine (bore 93 mm x stroke 110 mm) with a hemispherical cylinder head and had a pre-selector Wilson gearbox. They were robust but heavy weighing over 700 kgs and had a top speed of 260 km/h and were driven by French privateers Louis Rosier, Pierre "Levegh," Philippe Etancelin and Yves Giraud-Cabantous plus Johnny Claes from Belgium. Finally there was Gordini with his 4-cylinder 1430 cc cars which when fitted with a supercharger became very unreliable and in terms of speed were completely outclassed (140 bhp and 220 km/h). Frenchmen Maurice Trintignant and Robert Manzon struggled with them as best they could!

On 26th May an F2 race was held in pouring rain on the Borély Park circuit, which was won by Villoresi. Ascari finished second just 1/10s behind and then came Fangio and Sommer in Ferrari 166s. On Easter Monday 10th April there was the traditional event in Pau open to F1 cars. Victory went to Fangio in his

P. MENARD

Designer: Gioacchino Colombo

Engine

Make/type: Ferrari 125
No. of cylinders: 60° V12
Cubic capacity: 1496.7 (two stage supercharging)
Bore/stroke: 55 x 52.5 mm
Compression ratio: 7:1
Max. power: 280 bhp
Max. revs: 8000 rpm
Block: light alloy/steel cylinder linings
Carburettors: 1 Weber 40 DO 3 C
Distribution: 2x 2 D.O.H.C
No. of valves per cylinder: 2
Ignition: 2 magnetos
No. of plugs per cylinder: 1

Transmission

Gearbox/ no/ of ratios: Ferrari (4) + reverse (Monaco 5+ reverse)
Clutch: single plate

Chassis

Type: Tubular steel beams and cross braces
Suspension: Double wishbones, lower transversal springs, front/de
Dion rear with two semi-elliptic springs, rear
Shock absorbers: Houdaille hydraulic levers
Wheels: spoked Borranis
Tyres: Pirelli 5.50 x 16 (Front) / 6.50 x 16 (Rear)
Brakes: drums on all four wheels

Dimensions

Wheelbase: 2380 mm
Tracks: 1278 mm (Front) / 1250 mm (Rear)
Fuel tank: 140 litres
Dry weight: 560 kgs

Used in Monaco and Switzerland in 1950 and in half-a-dozen
non-championship events in 1949-50.

4 CLT/48 Maserati entered by the Argentinian team from Villoresi's Ferrari while Ascari's went out on lap 10 with a broken rear axle. On 16th April the San Remo Grand Prix saw the first appearance of the 158 Alfa Romeos a single example of which was entered for Fangio making his debut for the Italian team. Ascari was on pole with Fangio setting the second quickest time. Alberto jumped into an immediate lead then spun handing first place to the Alfa Romeo. The Italian set off like a bat out of hell to make up lost ground but crashed out for good on lap 33. Juan Manuel went on to score his first victory for Alfa Romeo driving a brilliant race on a track made slippery by rain. His win also silenced the chauvinistic Italian press, which had wanted another Italian driver alongside the two Fs.

The world championship finally got under way on 13th May with the British Grand Prix on the Silverstone circuit but without Ferrari! In fact, the Scuderia had chosen to race in an F2 event in Belgium attracted by the large sums of money on offer. Or was it due to the fact that like Bugatti in the 1925 French Grand Prix Enzo Ferrari did not want to see his cars beaten into a cocked hat by the Alfa Romeos? In the absence of the Scuderia Alfa Romeo had no opposition as the Talbots and Maseratis were completely outclassed. Farina scored an easy win from team-mate Luigi Fagioli while Fangio retired. The works Ferraris were on hand for the second round of the championship in Monaco with three cars for Ascari, Villoresi and an older model for Sommer. This race also saw the Grand Prix

• **50**_ Monaco 21ˢᵗ May 1950: This race really marked the start of the world championship as the first round on the Silverstone circuit had been dominated by Alfa Romeo in the absence of Ferrari. Ascari in his 125 C was one of the few drivers to escape the huge pile-up on the first lap in the Bureau de Tabac corner. He finished second. *(Maniago collection)*

debut of another Argentinian backed by the national Automobile Club, Froilan Gonzalez in a 4 CLT/48 Maserati. The tubby Gonzalez quickly became known as the Pampas Bull and was extremely quick as proved by his third place on the grid for his first Grand Prix in 1m 53.7s behind the Alfas driven by Fangio (1m 50.2s and Farina (1m 52.8s) but ahead of Villoresi (1m 54.3s) and Ascari (1m 54.8s). The Ferraris were on the third row behind Etancelin's Talbot and Fagioli's Alfetta, which turned out to be a blessing in disguise. On lap 1 Farina crashed in the Bureau de Tabac corner sparking off a massive pile up that led to the elimination of ten cars. The track was awash with fuel but luckily there was no fire. Fangio threaded his way through the wreckage and went on to score the first of his twenty-four F1 world championship victories. Ascari too drove an intelligent race and when Villoresi retired took over second place, which he held to the chequered flag notching up six points.

Farina won the Swiss Grand Prix on the Berne circuit on 4ᵗʰ June from Fagioli and set fastest lap tightening his grip on the championship. The Ferrari 125 Cs now had a new de Dion rear axle and a 4-speed gearbox. When Ascari returned to Maranello after the Monaco race he explained to Enzo Ferrari that he was unable to sign autographs for pretty girls as the palm of his right hand was in ribbons because of the stiffness of the gearbox! Enzo took him seriously and shelved the old 5-speed version. It did not make much difference as the two Ferraris started from the second row behind the Alfas in the hands of Fangio, Farina and Fagioli and retired early on, Ascari on lap 4 with an oil leak and Villoresi on lap 9 with broken transmission. Then for the Belgian event Ferrari brought along a new car designated the 275. It was powered by an unsupercharged 3.3 litres engine (275 ccs3 unitary capacity) and was the first of the evolutions programmed by Lampredi. Ascari

had already driven a sports car in the Mille Miglia powered by a similar engine (72 x 68 mm bore and stroke giving 3322 ccs). In F1 trim it put out 280 bhp and was much more flexible than the supercharged version. Practice was again dominated by the 158s with Farina setting pole in 4m 43s. Fangio recorded the same time but after the doctor. Fagioli completed an all Alfa front row with a lap in 4m 43s. Villoresi was on row 2 in 4m 47s with Sommer's Talbot in 4m 48s. Ascari was sixth quickest in 4m 49s and was obviously not going to be a front-runner. Fangio scored a runaway win from Fagioli after Farina's retirement but Sommer managed to put his lumbering Talbot in the lead for a few laps when the Alfa Romeos had to refuel proving that Lampredi was on the right track. It should be pointed out that the Frenchman was the first to advise Ferrari and his engineer to go for an unsupercharged V12. Ascari came home fifth scoring two more championship points.

and did not score. The provisional championship standings were Fangio first with 26 points followed by Fagioli 24 and Farina 22. Enzo Ferrari had decided to give the French race a miss and invest all his efforts in preparation for the Italian Grand Prix so Ascari (8 points) and Villoresi (0) just had to grin and bear it!

The next round of the world championship was on the Monza circuit on 3rd September and in the meantime there was an F1 race on the Planques circuit in Albi on 16th July run in two heats. Ascari back behind the wheel of a 125 C finished ninth in the first heat won by Sommer's Talbot and retired in the second, which went to Gonzalez in his Maserati. Louis Rosier (Talbot) won the event on the addition of times. A week later the Frenchman scored a more telling victory in the Dutch Grand Prix on the Zandvoort circuit from Villoresi (125 C/49) and Ascari (F2 166). The 'Grand Prix des Nations" took place on 30th July and Lampredi used the race to pursue the development of the unsupercharged Ferrari. Although it was a non championship event it attracted a first-class entry that included four Alfettas, eight 4 CLT/48 Maseratis, three Talbots etc. The Scuderia brought along its new 340 F1 for Ascari. With the bore increased from 72 to 80 mm the overall cubic capacity was now 4101 ccs and power had risen to 320/330 bhp. Villoresi was entrusted with the 275 F1 driven by Ascari in Belgium. In practice Alberto got round in 1m 48.7s good enough for second place on the grid although two seconds slower than Fangio's pole in the 158 Alfa Romeo. Villoresi then equalled his team-mate's time to put both of the big Ferraris on the front row. In the race Ascari held second for a long time in Fangio's wake but a broken valve damaged a piston and he crawled home in fourth place some six laps behind the Alfa Romeos of Fangio, de Graffenried and Taruffi. Villoresi, unfortunately, had a big accident in the 275. He slid off on oil and the car went over a protective barrier killing three spectators and injuring twenty. Gigi himself was badly hurt in the accident and was out of action for several weeks.

On 20th August Ascari put on a scintillating performance in the German Grand Prix for F2 (2 litres unsupercharged) cars. He scored an easy win in an F2 166 ahead of the Simca-Gordinis of Frenchmen Simon and Trintignant. It was a God-given opportunity to learn the long and dangerous 22.870 km Nürburgring and would pay dividends a year later. Next on his agenda was the International Trophy on the Silverstone circuit

• 52_ A legendary trio snapped in 1950. From left to right: Alberto Ascari, Aurelio Lampredi and Enzo Ferrari in typical clothing that would not look out of place in a film by Vittorio de Sica. They were plotting the 4.5 litres 375 F1. *(Ferrari factory archives)*

On the Reims circuit on 2nd July the Argentinian was again unbeatable in the torrid conditions reigning in champagne land. He set pole and fastest lap and won as he pleased from Fagioli who racked up yet another second place. Farina was delayed by gremlins in the ignition

• **54**_ London August 1950: Ascari and Serafini, who had come to race at Silverstone, met up with their old friend Tazio Nuvolari (on the right). The three former Bianchi riders were invited to a party by the English agent for the make. *(Bianchi factory archives)*

(Archives Christian Bedei)

Louis Klemantaski

Louis Klemantaski was well known for, among other things, having taken part in the Mille Miglia as Peter Collins's co-driver on a few occasions in an Aston Martin and then in a Ferrari. He took some photos from the cockpit, which rank among the most extraordinary shots in the history of racing. He was a motor racing photographer for many years and rubbed shoulders with the greats of his era. In 1998, he told us this story in his home in England, which typifies the golden age of motor sport:

"I was lucky enough to get to know Ascari well. In August 1950 I was coming back from a race on the Nürburgring that he'd won. The International Trophy was being held at Silverstone the following weekend with a sports car race as a curtain raiser. Rodney Walkerley, the chief editor of the sports section of the Motor, was bringing me back in his car. We saw Ascari and Serafini at the bar on the ferry. I went up to them and introduced myself. We spoke a little in French when Ascari sighed and said to me:' We have to go to London. Tell me the way.' I began explaining it to him when suddenly he exclaimed. 'Why don't you come with me?' I said 'OK that'd be great.' When we arrived in Dover I went up to the two open Ferrari 166 MMs. I made to get into the passenger's seat and Ascari asked me: "In England you drive on the wrong side of the road. Right? Then drive the car!' And so we set off with me driving Ascari followed by Serafini in the other 166 MM. What a responsibility. At one moment I must've been doing 160 km/h; there was no speed limit and no traffic. Then I saw Ascari getting a bit worked up but I was doing nothing wrong so I gave him a questioning look. He showed me the gear lever knob and made the figure five with his fingers. I had never driven a car with five speeds before. I changed up into fifth and he went to sleep!"

where he drove the 125 C purchased by Tony Vandervell, the thinwall bearings manufacturer and future constructor of the Vanwall. Ascari had won the race the previous year but this time he retired with mechanical problems. Some compensation came in the form of victory in the sports car event.

Louis Klemantaski, the famous photographer, tells an amusing story about Ascari at that time (see insert).

Official practice for the Italian Grand Prix began on 1st September. Alfa Romeo brought no fewer than five cars to Monza for Fangio, Farina, Fagioli, Sanesi and Taruffi while Ferrari entered just two but they were the completely new 375 F1s. After the intermediate 4.1 litres version Lampredi had increased the cubic capacity to 4.5 litres (4493 ccs) by lengthening the stroke from 68 to 74.5 mm. This gave the car a power output of between 340 and

• **56**_ Monza 1st September 1950 during practice for the Italian Grand Prix. Aurelio Lampredi, on the left) and Enzo Ferrari with Ascari and Frederico Giberti (on the right in dark glasses). *(Maniago collection)*

350 bhp. Ascari drove one and the other was entrusted to Serafini as Villoresi was still convalescing after his accident. Whitehead entered his private 125 and there were eight Maseratis, seven Lago-Talbots, two Simca-Gordinis, a Jaguar-engined Ferrari and an ERA. The battle for victory was obviously down to a straight fight between Alfa Romeo and Ferrari. Fangio drew first blood by setting pole in his 158 in 1m 58.3s only 1/10s quicker than Ascari. They were the only two drivers to break the two-minute barrier and sharing the front row with them were Farina (2m 00.1s) and Sanesi (2m 00.2s). Then came Fagioli, Serafini, Taruffi and Sommer's Talbot some 10 seconds slower than Fangio. The excitement in the crowd reached fever pitch as the flag dropped. The three Alfa Romeos were quickest off the mark with Farina leading Fangio and Sanesi but Ascari was giving nothing away and soon sliced past the latter two and began to harry Giuseppe showing the speed of the 375 F1. On lap 14 he took the lead only to be repassed two laps later by Farina. Still Alberto hung on until lap 20 when a blown valve forced him out. Serafini was down in third place behind Fagioli and ahead of Sommer. When he came in to refuel on lap 48 he handed over to Ascari. Farina then stopped for fuel but such was his lead that he went back out still in first place. Fangio had retired and in seond was now Fagioli some 2m 30s behind Farina but only 15s ahead of Ascari. Alberto really got the hammer down and passed Fagioli to score a brilliant second place on the 375 F1's maiden outing. Farina bagged the 8 points for victory and became the first ever F1 World Champion with 30 points from Fangio with 28. Ascari was classified fifth with 11 points but Alfa Romeo could sense that the 'times, they were a-changing!'

There was one race left on the F1 calendar, albeit a non-championship event, the Penya-Rhin Grand Prix on the Pedrables-Barcelona circuit. Alfa Romeo did not send any cars but there was a newcomer in the form of two of the ear-splitting V16 BRMs. The Scuderia entered three cars, a pair of 375s for Ascari and Serafini and a 340 for the Italian all-rounder Piero Taruffi. They finished one, two, three well ahead of Etancelin's Talbot and de Graffenried's Maserati. Both BRMs retired. Thus, the season finished on a high note for Ascari.

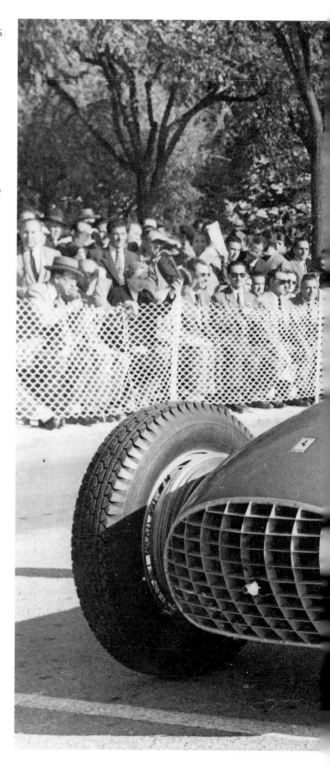

In F2 the 166s continued to rack up victories and Alberto added another one to his tally after Modena, Rome, Reims and the Nürburgring on the 'lac de Garde' circuit from Serafini. In sports cars he won the Luxemburg Grand Prix from Villoresi and both signed up with Ferrari for the 1951 season. Taruffi and

Gonzalez joined the Scuderia while in the Alfa Romeo camp Fangio, Farina and Fagioli had their contracts extended and Sanesi and Bonetto also drove for the team on an occasional basis. The Portello firm continued the developement of the Alfettas with the adoption of a de Dion rear end and increased the power output to 425 bhp. At Ferrari Lampredi began work on a twin ignition version of the 375 F1, which was expected to give over 380 bhp. Ferrari reduced its F2 programme while enlarging its sports car activities with the 4.1 litres 340. 1951 was going to be a busy year for drivers and mechanics. ■

Chapter 9

1951 A World Champion in the making

Ascari and Villoresi were great friends outside racing and when Gigi, now fully recovered from his accident in Switzerland, asked Alberto to accompany him in a Lancia Aurelia saloon in the Sestrières rally he accepted immediately. Contrary to the previous year neither driver was competing in the Temporada so they did not see Mercedes-Benz bringing its old 1939 cars out of mothballs (one was entrusted to Fangio) only to be trounced in two F. Libre races in Buenos Aires by Gonzalez's 2-litres Ferrari. They won the Sestrières rally run in February on snow-bound roads while awaiting the start of the European season and it is probable that their victory attracted the attention of Gianni Lancia who was planning his company's return to racing at the highest level.

The first event of any significance was held on the Syracuse circuit on 11th March. The new 5.4 km circuit had to be covered eighty times and opposition to Ascari and Villoresi's 375 F1s (backed up by Serafini in a 2.6 litres 212) came from the 4 CLT/48 Maseratis of Farina, Schell and Bira plus Rosier and Louveau's Talbots. Ascari set pole ahead of Farina and went straight into a lead he held until lap 69 when his engine blew. Victory went to Villoresi and the same scenario was repeated at Pau on 26th March. Even on the very tight French circuit hardly tailored to the needs of the big Ferrari Ascari again set pole at almost 100 km/h in a time of 1m 41.8s from Villoresi and Serafini in the 212. When the flag fell he again went to the front and opened up a large

gap, set the fastest lap as at Syracuse, and then hit transmission problems just before half-distance. So again Villoresi took over first place and scored another easy win from Rosier's Talbot and Farina's Maserati.

Finally at San Remo on 22nd April his luck turned. The Italian circuit was similar to Pau in many respects and after almost three hours racing Ascari, who started from pole and set fastest lap, saw the chequered flag in the new twin plug version of the 375 F1. Into second came Serafini in the older 375 F1 with single ignition while Villoresi retired after an accident. Third place fell to Swiss independent Rudi Fischer in his 2.6 litres Ferrari ahead of Schell's Maserati and Moss's F2 HWM. It was an encouraging win for the team despite Alfa Romeo's absence.

On 29th April the Scuderia entered four cars for the Mille Miglia run over a 1600 km layout. They were all 340 Americas and their 4.1 litres engine put out between 230 and 240 bhp. The drivers were Ascari, Serafini, Villoresi and Vittorio Marzotto one of the scions of a rich textile family and lovers of motor racing as well as Ferrari clients since the company's birth. Giannino, entered in a 212 Export, won the 1953 Mille Miglia in a 340 MM. This event saw the debut of a young Italian called Eugenio Castellotti in a 166 MM Ferrari. Victory went to Villoresi while Ascari's race ended in a serious accident. He set off from Brescia at around 4 a.m. in the dark and some forty kilometres further on he was blinded by the headlights of a spectator's car as

• **59**_ In the San Remo Grand Prix on 22nd April 1951 Ascari scored a promising victory in the 375 F1 as well as setting fastest lap. Serafini finished 2nd in another 375 F1 while Villoresi crashed out in the third Ferrari.
(Maniago collection)

the person had turned them on to read the races numbers! There was a pool of oil on the entry to a corner and Ascari slid off hitting a spectator who died soon afterwards. The C-Type Jaguars in the hands of Stirling Moss and Leslie Johnston also went off in the same spot for the same reason, fortunately without injury to drivers or spectators. After the accident legal action was taken against Ascari but he was aquitted following eyewitness reports and the arguments he put forward in his defence. However, he was deeply upset by this incident and refused to race in the event for the next two years. His difficult start to the season continued as he crashed in the Marseille F2 race when overtaking a tail-ender who suddenly swerved straight in front of him. Then in the Christopher Columbus Grand Prix in Genoa on 20th May he realised that his fuel tank was leaking and came in for a refill. He rejoined but a little further on his car caught fire. He stopped without difficulty and while he was jumping out of the car he caught his foot in the steering wheel. Biondetti came to his help and although Ascari managed to extract himself he received second-degree burns to his right-hand forearm.

On 5th May Alfa Romeo entered two cars for the International Trophy on the Silverstone circuit. Fangio won his heat and Farina the second but the final was stopped after the track was flooded by a storm and victory went to the Thinwall Special, a 375 Ferrari driven by Reg Parnell, bought from the factory by Tony Vandervell. Contrary to previous years there were no works Ferraris entered for this event.

On 27th May the Swiss Grand Prix, the opening round of the 1951 F1 World Championship, was held on the Berne Bremgarten circuit in drizzling rain which only served to make the track even more dangerous for the cars and drivers who had to cover 42 laps of the circuit, some 305 kms. Fangio set pole in 2m 31.9s ahead of his team-mate Farina in 2m 37.8s and Villoresi in the first of the Ferraris in 2m 39.3. The second row was made up of Sanesi and de Graffenried in their Alfa Romeos in 2m 40.3s and 2m 41.8s respectively. Ascari – still handicapped by his burns - could do no better than row three with a lap in 2m 46s behind Taruffi whose best was 2m 45.2s and Rosier's Talbot in 2m 52.7s. There were wide gaps between the two quickest Alfas and the Ferraris as well as between the Italian cars

and the rest of the field. Fangio jumped straight into the lead while Farina started with full tanks (around 300 litres) hoping to cover the full distance without refuelling, as the race was shorter than usual and also slower due to the rain. However, he was not up to coping with the sheer physical demands of his very heavy car and saw his chances of victory go up in smoke. He did manage to cling onto second fending off Sanesi and Villoresi in the first of the Ferraris. Ascari was sixth behind de Graffenried and was soon overtaken by Taruffi who was very much at home in the wet as he then passed de Graffenried, Sanesi and Farina by the end of the race to finish second. Ascari's sixth place did not give him any points while Fangio pocketed eight plus one for the fastest lap putting him into the championship lead.

• **60_** Berne-Bremgarten 27th May 1951: Fangio won the Swiss Grand Prix in atrocious conditions in his Alfetta. Taruffi saved Ferrari's honour with a second place. Ascari was still suffering from burns received in an F2 race a week earlier in Genoa and struggled home sixth.
(Maniago collection)

• **61**_ A rare colour shot of
Ascari and his close friend and
mentor Villoresi. In this case
the pupil surpassed the master.
(Ferrari factory archives)

Belgium welcomed round three on 17th June (the Indy 500 having taken place on May 30th) on the Spa-Francorchamps circuit. This time the distance was much longer, 36 laps of the 14.120 km circuit, a total of 508 kms. It was fine and sunny in the Ardennes and the drivers were able to go pedal to metal leading to increased fuel consumption. This factor obviously played into Ferrari's hands, as their normally aspirated engine was much less thirsty than the supercharged one powering the Alfas. The Scuderia reckoned on making one stop fewer than their rivals and it also started the race with less fuel on board. Villoresi was again quickest of the 375 F1s in 4m 29s which put him on the front row alongside Farina and Fangio (on pole) in their Alfettas in 4m 28s and 4m 25s respectively. Ascari in 4m 30s and Taruffi in 4m 32s were on the second row. At the end of lap 1 Villoresi was in the lead from Farina, Ascari and Fangio followed by Taruffi and Sanesi. The Ferraris were able to exploit their weight advantage but after a few laps Fangio passed Ascari and on lap 9 Villoresi stopped because of an oil leak followed on lap 10 by Taruffi with a broken rear axle. This left Ascari to do battle with the Alfa Romeos even if Villoresi rejoined. Fangio set the fastest lap in 4m 22.1s a speed of 193.941 km/h and

when Farina came in to refuel on lap 14 he went into the lead. Not for long as when he pitted in turn on lap 15 and his mechanics found that the left-hand rear wheel was blocked and he lost almost fifteen minutes as his mechanics cut off the tyre and replaced it. He displayed Olympian calm even though it was the end of his victory hopes. Farina took the chequered flag from Ascari and Villoresi after Sanesi's retirement. Alberto finished 2m 51s behind the Alfetta knowing that he was unable to match the Portello car's pace on the very quick Belgian layout.

The Le Mans 24-Hours race took place on the weekend of 23rd-24th June without the works Ferraris the Scuderia being represented by privateers. Ascari, Villoresi and Taruffi had the weekend off and victory in the Sarthe went to the C-Type Jaguar in the hands of Peter Whitehead and Peter Walker while most of the Ferraris were eliminated by mechanical problems. The best the 1949 winner Luigi Chinetti could do was eighth in a 340.

The French or ACF Grand Prix was held on 1st July on the very fast (190 km/h average for the quickest) Reims-Gueux circuit where Froilan Gonzalez made his official debut for the Ferrari team after starting the season in a Lago-Talbot as Taruffi gave this race and the following one a miss. Ascari was third quickest in practice in 2m 28.1s which put him on the front row together with Farina in 2m 27.4s and Fangio who again set pole in 2m 25.7s. The Grand Prix itself was run over a distance of 77 laps of the 7.815 km circuit, a total of 601 kms, the longest ever for an F1 race. The Alfa Romeos were on a three stopper for tyres and fuel as against just one for the Ferraris! Fangio and Ascari were locked in battle right from the start and Alberto shot past the Argentinian as the cars roared through the start/finish area at the end of lap 1. Villoresi had passed Sanesi and Gonzalez had done the same to Farina. Each time round Fangio, Acari and Farina lowered the lap record as Alberto was now in the lead and Giuseppe had clawed his way up to second place. On lap 9 gearbox problems forced Ascari into retirement allowing Farina into the no.1 spot. Fangio too had to stop to have his ignition adjusted which lost him precious time and eventually caused his retirement. Alfa Romeo stopped Fagioli and told him to hand over to

the Argentinian on lap 24. Ferrari did the same with Gonzalez in second place on lap 34 and he relinquished his 375 F1 to Ascari. So battle was again joined between the two number ones. Fangio came home first ahead of Ascari sharing the eight points for victory with Fagioli to which he added one for fastest lap while Alberto took home three as did Gonzalez. Farina finished fifth adding a mere two to his tally. After the French race the championship positions were: 1st Fangio (15 points, 2nd Farina (14) and 3rd Ascari (9).

Next on the calendar was the British Grand Prix on 14th July on the Silverstone circuit, a race that has gone down in history. The focal point of interest for the British spectators was the debut of the V16 BRMs in a race counting for the F1 World Championship. It was also the first time that a Ferrari was on pole position in the competition's history. This honour fell to Gonzalez who took to the Silverstone layout like a duck to water lapping in 1m 43.4s, an average speed of 101.318 mph,

• **62_** Reims 1st July 1951: The legendary Charles Faroux is about to give the start of the ACF Grand Prix. Ascari's Ferrari is on the outside of the front row with Fangio's 159 Alfetta (n°.4) and Farina in n°.2. Both teams were hit with mechanical problems. Victory went to Fangio in Fagioli's car while Ascari came second in Gonzalez's.

• **63**_ Silverstone 14th July 1951: A red-letter day in motor racing history. Ascari looks a bit worried before the start of the British Grand Prix because of his team-mate Gonzalez's speed as the latter has snatched pole from Fangio's Alfa Romeo. That day the Pampas Bull gave Ferrari its maiden victory in the Formula 1 World Championship while Alberto was forced out with gearbox problems.

the first time the 100 mph barrier was broken on the English circuit. He was a full second ahead of Fangio, 1.6s quicker than Farina and 2s faster than Ascari. In practice the Italian complained that his brakes were not good enough to which Gonzalez replied that he only had to hit the pedal harder! The two Ferraris and two Alfa Romeos shared the front row of the grid and behind them came Villoresi, Sanesi and Felice Bonetto. And it was the Italian veteran Bonetto, replacing Fagioli that day in the fourth Alfa, who made the best start. Fangio made a cautious getaway while Gonzalez latched onto the leading Alfa's rear wheels. Ascari was back in fourth. On lap 2 Froilan sliced past the 158 and Alberto got the better of Farina. Two laps later Fangio nipped past Felice and set about Gonzalez whom he passed on lap 10, the same lap on which Ascari overtook Bonetto. After twenty laps the two Argentineans were separated by only five seconds and had drawn away from their pursuers led by Ascari with Farina glued to his tail. Gonzalez, arms pistoning up and down,

pulled in his fellow-countryman whom he hustled past on lap 39. On lap 56 Ascari's gearbox broke robbing him of the chance of scoring Ferrari's first F1 world championship win. When Gonzalez came in for his final refuelling stop he sportingly offered his seat to the Ferrari no.1 saying they could share the eight points that went with victory. Alberto declined and told him to get back in and finish the job. Which he did giving Ferrari the first of a long string of successes in the World Championship. Ascari saw that Gonzalez deserved the win and furthermore he did not like the system of points sharing which disappeared in 1958. In addition, he wanted to score his first F1 victory single-handed. And his wish was soon to be fulfilled.

The next round of the championship was on the 22.180 km Nürburgring on 29th July with its 176 corners and it was there that Ascari gave an awesome display of his talent. He was very quick straight out of the box thanks to his 1950 win in F2 which helped him to find his marks on the track and in addition, he was now

• **64_** Nürburgring 28th July
1951: This time Ascari was on
pole ahead of Fangio and
Gonzalez. On the eve of the
German Grand Prix the three
drivers met up for a chat in the
Sporthotel bar. A happy
Aurelio Lampredi (on the left)
looks on as two of his Ferraris
are in front of the Alfas on the
grid.
(Barth Volker archives)

absolutely sure that the 375 F1s had the
beating of the Alfettas. He set pole in 9m 55.8s
from Gonzalez whose best was 9m 57.5s and
Fangio making his debut on the 'Ring lapped in
9m 59s. They were the only three to break the
10-minute barrier. Farina was on the outside of
the front row in 10m 01s. On the second was
Villoresi (10m 06.6s) Taruffi back again in a
Ferrari (10m 12.9) and German veteran Paul
Pietsch chosen by Alfa Romeo for his
knowledge of the circuit. This time Ferrari really
seemed to have the upper hand but to the
Scuderia's surprise it was Fangio who blasted
through in the lead as the cars completed the
first lap followed by Ascari, Gonzalez, Farina
and Pietsch. The German then spun in the
Carousel losing several minutes restarting his
engine and a few laps later he had a big
accident from which he emerged miraculously
unhurt as his car somersaulted off the track.
Meanwhile up front Fangio and Ascari were
locked in a daggers drawn duel as the Italian
had covered his third lap in a mind-boggling
10m 0.1s and was now only 1.2s behind Fangio.
Two laps later he was in the lead and when the
Argentinian and Farina dived into the pits to
refuel he found himself 8.8s ahead of Gonzalez
in second place. Gradually the Ferraris'
stranglehold on the race tightened. The
Scuderia's task was made all the easier when
Farina retired on lap 8 with gearbox problems.
When Ascari came in to refuel at half-distance
Gonzalez went into the lead and the gap
between the two Ferraris was 52 seconds with
Fangio only 8.7s behind Ascari. When Froilan
refuelled in turn Ascari went back into the lead
with Fangio breathing down his neck. Beating
the lap record twice Juan Manuel retook the
lead. By now the hammering that the cars had
taken was beginning to make itself felt.
Gonzalez's Ferrari was delayed and Fangio's

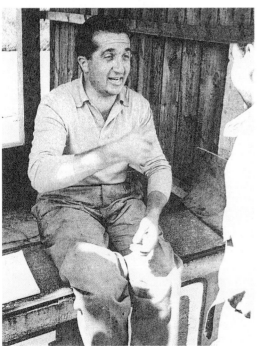

• **65 and 66_**
Nürburgring, 29th July 1951: A
calm-looking Ascari in the first
photo suddenly bursts into a
stream of voluble Italian in the
second.

85

• **67_** Just before the start of the German Grand Prix the Ferrari 375 F1s of Ascari (n°.71) Villoresi (n°.72) and Taruffi (n°.73) are lined up in front of the pits. Only Gonzalez's (n°.74) is missing. The Scuderia scored its second consecutive F1 World Championship win on the awesome Nürburgring with victory going to Ascari and all four cars were in the points. *(Barth Volker collection)*

Alfa's gearbox began playing up. Ascari came in for his final refuelling stop on lap 16 and also put fresh tyres on the rear, a cunning move as he had not pre-arranged this with his mechanics. He was able to ease off during the last four laps and took the flag to score the first of his thirteen F1 World Championship victories. Into second came Fangio 30.5s behind. It was the second consecutive defeat of Alfa Romeo by Ferrari and it would be the same story at Monza (see next chapter: A Memorable Race).

And so six weeks after Monza came the final round of the 1951 F1 World Championship, the Spanish Grand Prix on the F1 calendar for the first time on 28th October on the Pedrables Barcelona circuit. It was to prove decisive in the attribution of the title. In the meantime Ascari and Gonzalez scored a double in the Modena F2 Grand Prix Alberto driving the new 4-cylinder 500 F2 which would play a decisive role in 1952 and 53, while the Argentinian was at the wheel of an older 166. It was his third win in this category after the Monza Autodromo event in June plus Naples. In Maranello mechanics and engineers had plenty of time to ensure ultimate preparation of the cars for the decisive Spanish event.

When the teams arrived in Barcelona the press, mainly Italian and Spanish including the Sojit brothers for Argentinian radio who followed Fangio and Gonzalez's every move,

Designer : Aurelio Lampredi

Engine

Make/type : Ferrari 375
No. of cylinders: 60° V12
Cubic capacity: 4493.7 ccs
Bore/stroke: 80 x 74.5 mm
Compression ratio: 12:1
Max. power: 350 bhp (Monza 1951: 380 bhp)
Max. revs: 7500 rpm
Block: alloy
Carburettors: 3 Weber 46 DCFs
Distribution: 2x1 O.H.Cs
No. of valves per cylinder: 2
Ignition: 2 Marelli magnetos
No. of plugs per cylinder: 2

Transmission

Gearbox/no. of ratios: Ferrari: 4 + reserve
Clutch: multi plate

Chassis

Type: Rectangular tubes
Suspension: independent with double wishbones, transversal elliptic springs, front/ de Dion axle, transversal lower elliptic springs, two push rods, rear
Shock absorbers: Houdaille hydraulic
Wheels: spoked Borranis
Tyres: 5.50 x 16 (Front) / 7.50 x 17 (Rear) (Spain 1951: 7.50 x 16) Pirellis
Brakes: drums on all four wheels

Dimensions

Wheelbase: 2410 mm
Tracks: 1278 mm (Front) / 1250 mm (Rear)
Fuel tank: 195 litres
Dry weight: 780 kgs

Used in Italy (1950) and from Switzerland to Spain in 1951, Indianapolis 1952 and in several non-championship events in 1951-52.

• **68**_ During the race Ascari gave his mechanics a bit of a fright when he came in for an unscheduled stop to change wheels. He was well in the lead but Fangio was making a last desperate attempt to catch him. Before the race he was told of von Brauchitsch's misfortune in 1935 when his tyre blew on the last lap allowing Tazio Nuvolari to score one of his greatest victories in his Alfa Romeo.
(Barth Volker archives)

• **69**_ Ascari takes the chequered flag from Fangio's Alfa Romeo to win the first of his thirteen F1 World Championship Grands Prix.
(Barth Volker archives)

• **70**_ Pedbarles/Barcelona 28th October 1951: Ascari finishes fourth in his 375 F1 in the Spanish Grand Prix. Due to a wrong wheel choice the Scuderia Ferrari blew its chances of beating the Alfa Romeos in the final round of the championship.

had whipped the spectators up to fever pitch. The Pedrables circuit probably had the widest start and finish straight in the whole of the world championship and the track measured 6.316 kms using part of the famous Avenue Diagonal. The race was scheduled for seventy laps, a distance of 442.120 kms. It was also the first time that timing to one hundredth of a second was used in the world championship while spectator protection was enough to send shivers down one's spine. The grid lined in 4,3,4,3 formation and pole fell to Ascari in 2m 10.59s some 1.68/100th of a second quicker than Fangio. Gonzalez and Farina completed the front row. On row 2 were Villoresi's Ferrari, de Graffenried's Alfa Romeo and Taruffi's Ferrari. The pack was released under a scorching sun and Ascari made the best getaway followed by Farina and Fangio. Juan Manuel quickly nipped past the Doctor and began to hassle Ascari and by lap 4 he was leading the dance. Ferrari, though, was to lose the race through an error of judgement. The day before the race the Scuderia decided to fit 16 inch wheels instead of the normal 17 inch ones and the former were totally unable to cope with the heat and the pounding they received on the long straight. The team had reckoned on doing the race without refuelling but on lap 6 Taruffi came in with his tyres in tatters followed by Villoresi on lap 8, Ascari on lap 9 and finally Gonzalez. It was the end for Ferrari and at half-distance Fangio and Farina

led in their Alfa Romeo 159s from Gonzalez, Villoresi and Ascari. Luigi retired and Gonzalez managed to snatch second place from Farina when the latter refuelled for a second time. Fangio came home an easy winner and also set fastest lap assuring himself of the first of his five F1 world championship titles. His final total was 31 points out of 37 scored while a very disappointed Ascari finished second with 25 (28). Although at the end of their development the Alfas had shown that they were still a force to be reckoned with and Fangio's success was a well-deserved one. In the opinion of the pundits the Italian and the Argentinian were the best two drivers of the moment.

Epilogue: Before the Spanish Grand Prix Ascari and Fangio had agreed that whoever won the world championship would invite the runner-up to dinner. The latter would choose the restaurant and the guests. And so the following Thursday Juan Manuel hosted a dinner for Ascari and fifty friends in Savini's restaurant in Milan where a good time was had by all.

Ascari was given the honorary title of Italian athlete of the Year but already his mind had turned to 1952 and revenge. However he still had another race to come, the Carrera Panamerica in Mexico in November in which he drove a Ferrari Viginale Export coupe with his friend Villoresi. Taruffi and Chinetti were in a second 212 Export, as the Italo-American,

winner for the third time of the Le Mans 24 Hours race in 1949, had become the Ferrari importer for the USA. The Carrera was very important for advertising the make on the North American continent. In principle only touring cars were eligible for the event so Vignale produced a 4-seater coupe body to disguise the 212 Exports. This crazy race crossed Mexico from south to north over six days and consisted of eight stages totalling over 3 000 kms. To be in with a chance of winning a driver needed to combine speed, endurance and the improvisation of a rally man. Ferrari's first attempt was crowned with success as the team entered by Franco Cornacchia, the dealer for the make in Milan and manager of the Scuderia Guastalla, scored a double with Taruffi and Chinetti leading Ascari and Villoresi home after overcoming problems in the first stage when the Pirelli tyres threw treads. From the second onwards they used Mexican Goodyears, which were better able to cope with the heat and the surface. The Ferraris took the lead in the third stage and were never headed though it must be said that their only real opposition came from a Lancia Special as the remainder of the field consisted of big American saloons. The win made an enormous impact publicitywise and the Scuderia and its drivers shared a bonus of 37,000 dollars from which the costs of transporting the two cars from Italy to Mexico had to be deducted. Chinetti returned to New York and the other three went back to Italy by plane while the cars were sold to Mexicans. ■

Chapter 10
Triumph at Monza

• **73**_ Monza 16° September 1951: A lovely snap of the Ferrari 375 F1 in the Italian Grand Prix with a relaxed Ascari at the wheel on the way to his second victory of the season.

"A memorable race"
Italian Grand Prix
16th September 1951

B efore the Italian Grand Prix Fangio was leading the F1 World Championship ratings with 27 points from Ascari (17) and Farina and Gonzalez (15). The regulations specified that only the best four results would count towards the championship and there were still two rounds to go in Italy and Spain. Ascari had every chance of beating Fangio for the 1951 world title while Gonzalez and Farina were also potential candidates; and although their hopes of besting their team leaders were somewhat slim, they could still play a vital role in the outcome of the championship.

One can well imagine the ambience that reigned at Monza as the build up to the Grand Prix began because its results could be decisive in attributing the 1951 title. Given that Milan was within a stone's throw of the circuit the presence of a make from just beside the town itself provided an additional spark to light the *Tifosi's* fuse. Maranello had floored the make that had carried Italian colours for so many years on two consecutive occasions and in the respective teams were two Argentineans and four Milanese (two in each). Ferrari entered four works cars for Ascari, Villoresi, Taruffi and Gonzalez the same number as Alfa Romeo which entrusted its 159s to Fangio, Farina, Bonetto and de Graffenried called in at the last minute to replace Sanesi burnt in a testing accident. There was also a semi-works single plug 375 for Brazilian Chico Landi plus Peter Whitehead's supercharged 125 F1. The race also saw the first appearance of the F1 OSCA driven by Franco Rol. The car was powered by a 4.5 litres V12 engine designed by Gordini and built by the Maserati brothers. There were, however, no Maseratis. Making up the rest of the field were three Simca-Gordinis (Trintignant, Manzon and Simon) and six Lago-Talbots (Frenchmen Rosier, "Levegh" and

Giraud-Cabantous, Chiron from Monaco and Belgians Claes and Swaters) whose only hope was to pick up any crumbs that might fall from the rich men's table!

QUALIFYING

The Alfa Romeos were very much at home on this very quick circuit as had been the case at Spa and Reims so it was no surprise to see pole going to Fangio in 1m 53.2s (the first ever 200 km/h plus lap at Monza) from Farina in 1m 53.9s thanks to the latest evolution of the 159's engine ("M" for Migliorato) which put out 425 bhp. The best Ascari could do was 1m 55.1s and Gonzalez's 375 F1 completed the front row with a lap in 1m 55.9s. With two Alfa Romeos and two Ferraris on the front row it looked like a thrilling race in prospect but much would depend on fuel consumption and tyres. The Ferraris developed some 380 bhp at 7500 rpm and were lighter and less thirsty than their Portello rivals giving them an advantage in a race of over 500 kms.

STARTING GRID			
1. Fangio **1:53.2**	2. Farina 1:53.9	3. Ascari 1:55.1	4. Gonzalez 1:55.9
5. Villoresi 1:57.9	6. Taruffi 1:58.2	7. Bonetto 1:58.3	8. (Parnell) (2:02.9)
9. De Graffenried 2:05.2	10. (Richardson) (2:05.6)	11. Simon 2:08.0	12. Trintignant 2:08.9
13. Manzon 2:09.0	14. G-Cabantous 2:09.3	15. Rosier 2:10.8	16. (Landi) (2:11.3)
17. Chiron 2:12.1	18. Rol 2:13.4	19. Whitehead 2:16.0	20. Levegh 2:16.5
21. Claes 2:18.6	22. Swaters 2:18.8		

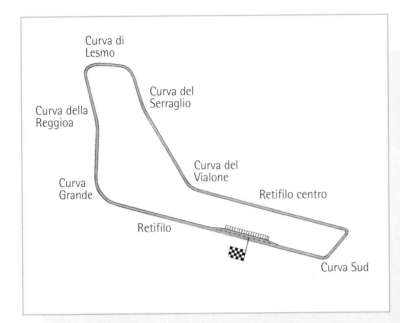

Curva di
Lesmo

Curva del
Serraglio

Curva della
Reggioa

Curva del
Vialone

Curva
Grande

Retifilo centro

Retifilo

Curva Sud

MONZA, THE CIRCUIT
Permanent circuit: 6.300 kms / 3.195 miles

The Italian Grand Prix on 3rd September 1922 inaugurated the Monza circuit in which FIAT scored a double (see chapter 3 of the present book). It has since become one of the Meccas of motor sport. All the great drivers have won there including Ascari (father and son), Nuvolari, Chiron, Caracciola, Fangio, Moss Hill (Phil and Graham), Clark, Stewart, Surtees, Lauda, Prost, Piquet, Senna and M. Schumacher. It consists of a banked section like Montlhéry and Brooklands and a road circuit laid out partially inside and partially outside the oval. The banked track was only used for records. Over the years various combinations have been tried for F1 and F2 Grands Prix and for sports car races like the Supercortemaghiore as well as prototypes (1000 kms) using half the oval and half the road circuit. The latter passed under the oval and sometimes it was possible to see cars racing parallel to each other in the link corners enabling drivers to judge their lead or the amount of ground to be made up. In any case, Monza is still a very fast circuit despite the installation of chicanes with high-speed curves and long straights where slip streaming plays a big role. In 1951, the Grand Prix was held on a 6.276 km layout to be covered 80 times, a total of 502.080 kms.

THE RACE

Given what was at stake it was maximum attack right from the start to the great joy of the huge crowd. The two Alfas in the hands of Fangio and Farina went straight into the lead ahead of Ascari who had fluffed his getaway. But by lap 2 he had already overtaken Farina and closed in on Fangio whom he passed a lap later sending the crowd into ecstasies. The early part of the race developed into a battle between the Ferrari and Alfa team leaders as de Graffenried and Farina were already in trouble with fuel feed problems. Things went from bad to worse in the Alfa camp when Fangio, who had retaken the lead, had to come in on lap 14 due to a thrown tyre tread. He went back out in fifth and at that moment there were three Ferraris in the first three places with Ascari leading Gonzalez and Villoresi. Fangio now had the bit between his teeth as he had nothing to lose and sliced past Bonetto and Villoresi. But at half-distance his engine cried enough (ignition) and he was obliged to watch the rest of the race from the pits. Ascari came home a triumphant winner from Gonzalez and Farina in third. The latter after taking over Bonetto's Alfa Romeo got as high as second when Gonzalez refuelled but a split fuel tank dashed his chances. Thus, Ferrari scored a double and Ascari's second victory put him in a strong position in the title chase as he now had 25 points only three behind Fangio (27) and ahead of Gonzalez (21) and Farina (18). Spain was to be the clincher. ■

• **74_** Just after the finish Ascari and his team manager Frederico Giberti get ready to drink the champagne to celebrate the Scuderia's success. Alberto's win on home ground ahead of Gonzalez sent the spectators into a frenzy of delight.

RESULTS – 80 race laps for 502.080 kms

1.	**Ascari**	**Ferrari**	**80**	**2:42:39.300**
				185.915 km/h
2.	Gonzalez	Ferrari	80	+ 44.600
3.	Farina/Bonetto	Alfa Romeo	79	1 lap
4.	Villoresi	Ferrari	79	1 lap
5.	Taruffi	Ferrari	78	2 laps
6.	Simon	Gordini	74	6 laps
7.	Rosier	Talbot-Lago	73	7 laps
8.	Giraud-Cabantous	Talbot-Lago	72	8 laps
NC.	Rol	Osca	67	13 laps

RETIREMENTS

Fangio	Alfa Romeo	39	Ignition
Manzon	Gordini	29	Engine
Trintignant	Gordini	29	Engine
Chiron	Talbot-Lago	23	Contact
Levegh	Talbot-Lago	9	Engine
Swaters	Talbot-Lago	7	Overheating
Farina	Alfa Romeo	6	Lubrication
Claes	Talbot-Lago	4	Cooling
De Graffenried	Alfa Romeo	1	Supercharger
Whitehead	Ferrari	1	Engine

FASTEST RACE LAP

Farina	Alfa Romeo	1:58.700
		191.070 km/h

LAP CHART

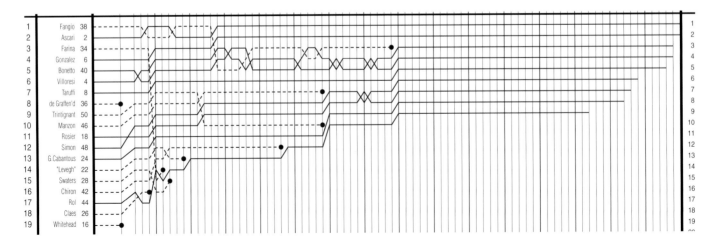

_ASCARI'S PERFORMANCE IN THE ITALIAN GRAND PRIX

YEAR	CIRCUIT	QUALIFYING	POSITION IN RACE	CAR
1947*	Milan	5th	5th	Maserati 4CL
1948*	Turin	7th	4th	Maserati 4CLT
1949*	Monza	**Pole**	**1st**	Ferrari 125 C
1950	Monza	2nd	Retired (valve)	Ferrari 375 F1
1951	Monza	3rd	**1st**	Ferrari 375 F1
1952	Monza	**Pole**	**1st**	Ferrari 500 F2
1953	Monza	**Pole**	Retired (accident)	Ferrari 500 F2
1954	Monza	2nd	Retired (valve)	Ferrari 625 F1

*Before the creation of the F1 World Championship.

75_ Silverstone 19th July 1952: Ascari downs a welcome drink after scoring the third of his six consecutive victories in the 1952 World championship in the British Grand Prix.

Chapter 11

1952
Ascari's
first World
Championship
Title

• **76**_ Turin 6th April 1952:
Ascari's bid for victory in the
Turin Grand Prix was
scuppered by a leak in his
Ferrari's oil tank. He came 5th in
a race won by Villoresi in
another modified 375 F1. This
was really a test before
Indianapolis.
(Collection Maniago)

Ascari, Villoresi and Taruffi resigned with
Ferrari for the 1952 season. Joining them
was the 1950 world champion, Giuseppe
Farina, in search of a seat following Alfa Romeo
withdrawal from racing. Portello's decision was
motivated by its desire to expand its road car
programme plus the government's refusal to
come up with state aid. It was to have far-
reaching consequences for the world
championship, as we shall see. In Maranello
development of the 375 F1 continued but other
constructors were not exactly in a hurry to build
new cars for the current formula. Matters were
probably not helped by the CSI's announcement
(the latter was the sporting arm of the FIA) that a
new formula would replace the present one in
1954 for cars with either 2.5 litres
unsupercharged engines or 750 cc supercharged
ones. Among the current constructors Maserati
did not envisage building a replacement for the
out-dated 4 CLT/48s, Osca did not have the
money to race its 4.5 litres V12 and the Lago-
Talbots had become collectors' items. The
Gordinis were completely outclassed and the V16
BRMs were still not ready, as the team had not
ironed out all the technical problems despite
having spent loads of money. The key race that
was to ring in the changes was the non-
championship Turin Grand Prix on 6th April 1952.
Victory went to Villoresi in his Ferrari 375 F1 and
yet again the BRMs failed to turn up. The CSI
foresaw a season dominated by Ferrari with tiny
grids and decided that only Formula 2 cars (2
litres unsupercharged and 750 ccs supercharged)
would be eligible to compete in the world
championship. It would certainly attract bigger
fields as Ferrari, Maserati, Osca, Gordini
(developing a 2-litres 6-cylinder car) the English
makes Cooper Bristol, Connaught and HWM and
the German AFMs and Veritas all had cars that
were eligible. Of course, some people claimed
that it was a bargain basement compromise with
less power and lower speeds, but on the other
hand it seemed certain that there would be close
racing between well known drivers in cars whose
performances were on a par with each other.
Finally, the running costs of an F2 were much
lower that those of an F1 thus it would attract
privateers as well. So the opening round, the
Swiss Grand Prix in Berne on 18th May, was
eagerly awaited. Lampredi had designed a
beautiful little 2-litres 4-clyinder car designated
the F2 500: it was compact and light, had a
power output of around 170 bhp and had
already proved itself to be a formidable weapon.
In the new car Ascari won the Syracuse Grand

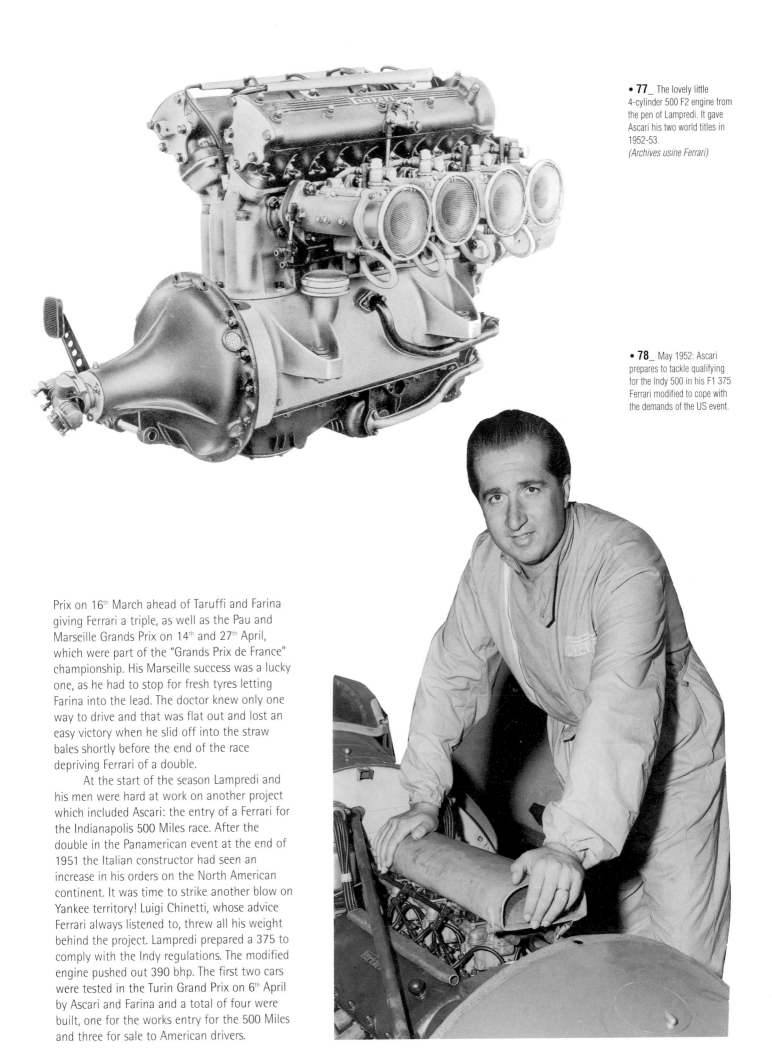

• **77_** The lovely little 4-cylinder 500 F2 engine from the pen of Lampredi. It gave Ascari his two world titles in 1952-53.
(Archives usine Ferrari)

• **78_** May 1952: Ascari prepares to tackle qualifying for the Indy 500 in his F1 375 Ferrari modified to cope with the demands of the US event.

Prix on 16th March ahead of Taruffi and Farina giving Ferrari a triple, as well as the Pau and Marseille Grands Prix on 14th and 27th April, which were part of the "Grands Prix de France" championship. His Marseille success was a lucky one, as he had to stop for fresh tyres letting Farina into the lead. The doctor knew only one way to drive and that was flat out and lost an easy victory when he slid off into the straw bales shortly before the end of the race depriving Ferrari of a double.

At the start of the season Lampredi and his men were hard at work on another project which included Ascari: the entry of a Ferrari for the Indianapolis 500 Miles race. After the double in the Panamerican event at the end of 1951 the Italian constructor had seen an increase in his orders on the North American continent. It was time to strike another blow on Yankee territory! Luigi Chinetti, whose advice Ferrari always listened to, threw all his weight behind the project. Lampredi prepared a 375 to comply with the Indy regulations. The modified engine pushed out 390 bhp. The first two cars were tested in the Turin Grand Prix on 6th April by Ascari and Farina and a total of four were built, one for the works entry for the 500 Miles and three for sale to American drivers.

For F1 regulars Indianapolis was a whole other world - which is still the case today over half-a-century later - both from a technical and sporting point of view. Qualifying was spread over a month and grid positions were decided not only by the times but also by the days on which they were set. Before this, however, every new driver had to pass his rookie test whatever his results. Ascari, Lampredi and their mechanics arrived in Indiana in the spring of 1952 four weeks before the race on 31st May which obliged Alberto to give the Swiss Grand Prix a miss. He was well paid for this sacrifice by Ferrari as at that time (and for long after) Enzo gave a very passable imitation of Scrooge in Charles Dickens's story "A Christmas Carol" when it came to parting

with money! Alberto passed his rookie test with flying colours. It consisted of covering a series of laps under the eyes of the USAC officials with the speed increasing by increments of 10 mph until the final one where no limit was imposed. The strips of adhesive tape on the tail of the car, which informed other drivers that a rookie was at the wheel, were then removed. It was more than a simple formality as it enabled newcomers to get to know the particularities of the Brickyard, which was laid out in the form of a rectangle with four rounded corners and was more difficult than it appeared at first glance. In 1952, some of the Indy Roadsters hit the 300 km/h mark on the straights and the quickest laps in qualifying already exceeded 220 km/h.

1952 German Grand Prix
Ferrari 500 F2

P. MÉNARD

Designer : Aurelio Lampredi

Engine
Make/type: Ferrari 500
No. of cylinders: straight 4 (front)
Cubic capacity: 1984.9 ccs (1953: 1997.1 ccs)
Bore & stroke: 90 x 78 mm (1953: 93 x 73.5 mm)
Compression ratio: 13:1
Max. power: 170 bhp (1953: 180 bhp)
Max. revs: 7200 rpm
Block: light alloy, steel cylinder liners
Carburettors: 2 Weber 45 DOEs
(1953: 2 Weber 52 DCOA – 3s)
Distribution: 2 O.H.C.s
No. of valves per cylinder: 2
Ignition: 2 magnetos
No. of plugs per cylinder: 2

Transmission
Gearbox/ no. of speeds: Ferrari longitudinal: 4 + reverse
Clutch: Ferrari multiplate

Chassis
Type: tubular with oval frame members and
rectangular cross sections (1953: steel tube ladder
frame)
Suspension: Front, double wishbone, lower leaf
springs/ Rear, de Dion, two parallel radius arms, lower
leaf spring
Shock absorbers: Houdaille vane type
Wheels; spoked Borranis
Tyres: 5.50 x 16 (1953: 5.25 x 16) (Front) / 6.00 x 16
(1953: 6.50 x 16) (Rear) Pirellis
Brakes: drums on all four wheels

Dimensions
Wheelbase: 2160 mm
Tracks: 1278 mm (Front) / 1250 mm (Rear)
Fuel tank capacity: 150 litres
Dry weight: 560 kgs (1953: 590 kgs)

Used from Belgium to Italy in 1952 and from
Argentina to Italy in 1953 plus more than
15 non-championship F2 races.

Ascari did his apprenticeship with his usual head-down concentration and did not lord it over the locals. He passed his rookie test in a disciplined, assured manner that forced the admiration of drivers like Agabashian, Nalon, Hanks, Vukovitch and Rathman who knew the track like the back of their hand. It is worth remembering that qualifying consisted of a series of four laps and not one as was - and is - current practice in F1. Ascari's initial attempts were pretty average. The Indy cars had 2-speed gearboxes and the drivers lifted off on entry to a corner and then hit the pedal on the exit. Alberto had a 4-speed box and changed down from fourth to third on entry and then reaccelerated on the exit but the car was not picking up speed quickly

enough. A few days before final qualifying he realised that a fuel feed problem was limiting power thus acceleration plus top speed. Lampredi only had a few days to find a solution. He rushed back to Italy by plane and returned from Maranello with a redesigned inlet manifold and three new 4-barrel Weber carburettors, which were a big improvement. Fortunately, it had rained during his absence and the other drivers had not improved their times. These modifications enabled Ascari to qualify his Ferrari in sixteenth place on the grid at an average speed of 216.147 km/h compared with Fred Agabashian's pole of 222.105 km/h in his diesel-power Kurtis Kraft. The Italian was counting on his car's better fuel consumption to gain places as only a single stop

• **79_** Indianapolis 30th May 1952: Ascari had begun to pick off his rivals one by one when on lap 41 he lost control of his car after the right-hand rear wheel collapsed. He managed to control the car, which came to a halt in the infield, ending his hopes of victory in the Brickyard.

• **80_** Spa-Francorchamps 1952: Ascari rounds the La Source hairpin on his way to his first Grand Prix victory in the 1952 world championship. It was the start of a series of nine consecutive successes, which no one has yet beaten!

for fuel was foreseen but tyre changes were also necessary. The team decided to stop at the 50, 100 and 150 lap mark (the race consisted of 200 laps). He made a cautious start keeping the revs under 6500 rpm as his plan was to use full power for the second part of the event. It took him around ten laps to gauge the track, his car and his rivals and then he began to up the pace and overtake his adversaries. On lap 41 when he was in ninth place the right-hand rear wheel of his Ferrari collapsed (broken hub) and the car ground to a halt in the infield. It was the end of the race for him but thanks to his uncanny mechanical sensitivity he had felt the break coming just before it did and stopped without problems or triggering off an accident. Great was the deception in the Ferrari camp. Alberto was congratulated after the race during prize giving. Everybody understood that without the breakage for which the driver was in no way responsible he could well have finished on the rostrum. It was to be his only Indy 500 even though in 1953 there was talk about a 3-litres V12 supercharged Ferrari for Ascari but it never appeared. In 1956, Farina failed to qualify in another car from the Prancing Horse stable.

In Europe Taruffi won the first round of the world championship in Switzerland in his F2 500 from Swiss privateer Rudi Fischer in another Ferrari and Jean Behra's Gordini. A week later Taruffi scored another victory in the Paris Grand Prix on the Montlhéry circuit which, although a non-championship event, attracted all the best drivers except Ascari. The fact that Enzo himself made one of his rare forays to a foreign country

showed that a lot was at stake. On 14th June Ascari was back with the Scuderia for the Le Mans 24 Hours race. He drove a 250 S with Villoresi and made a good start to the race beating the lap record but after three hours the clutch went.

• **81_** This shot shows off the beautiful lines of the F2 500 and also how close spectators were to the action in those far-off days. In the background the famous climb up "Eau Rouge" and Burneville can be seen in the rugged Ardennes countryside.

At Spa on 22nd June Ascari scored his first win in the 1952 championship. It was the start of a series of nine consecutive victories, a record that still stands today, despite the best efforts of Clark, Stewart, Lauda, Prost, Senna, Mansell and Schumacher. They were spread over two seasons and helped him to two successive world titles. It should be pointed out that his main rival Fangio was sidelined for the rest of 1952 after his accident at Monza at the beginning of June. Here follows the story of these nine wins in 1952 and 1953.

• **82_** The winner's spoils include a bouquet and a kiss. Ascari looks remarkably relaxed after 506 kilometres' racing most of it in the wet!

• **83**_ Brussels 26th June 1952: According to the Belgian importer's press release accompanying this photo, "Messrs Ascari and Farina stand beside the Jaguar that Mr. Ascari had just received at the headquarters of the Belgian Motor Company S.A." One wonders what Enzo Ferrari thought of this very opportunistic piece of publicity!

22nd June 1952: Belgian and European Grand Prix. 36 laps of the 14.080 km Spa-Francorchamps circuit: 506.880 kms. The twenty-two starters included three works Ferraris for Ascari, Taruffi and Farina plus private entries for Frenchman Louis Rosier and Belgian Charles de Tornaco. Following Fangio's Monza accident the works A6GCM Maseratis did not turn up as development had been suspended. On paper anyway opposition to the red cars came from the French Gordinis in 2-litres form for Behra and Manzon while Bira, Claes and O'Brien were in 1500 cc versions. Backing them up were the Alta-engined HWMs for team regulars Peter Collins and Lance Macklin plus Belgian guest drivers Paul Frère and Roger Laurent, the Cooper Bristols in the hands of Eric Brandon and Alan Brown plus young coming man Mike Hawthorn and Stirling Moss in the G-Type ERA with 6-cylinder Bristol power.

In practice Ascari set pole in 4m 37s three seconds quicker than Farina with Taruffi in 4m 46s completing the front row. Then came the works Gordinis in the hands of Behra and Manzon. At the end of lap 1 it was Behra who led to everybody's surprise having overtaken Taruffi first of all and then Farina and Ascari in Stavelot. He had a one second lead but by lap 2 Ascari was in front and Farina had also overtaken the plucky little Frenchman now locked in battle with Taruffi. On lap 14 rain began to fall and Taruffi lost control of his Ferrari and went off taking Behra with him, as the latter was glued to his tail. Luckily, neither driver was injured. This put the second works Gordini of Robert Manzon into third ahead of Mike Hawthorn very much at home in the tricky conditions. Ascari sailed away

to victory setting the fastest lap in the process. On lap 20 he was 38 seconds ahead of Farina. On lap 30 the gap was 1m 38s and at the finish it had stretched to 1m 57s. The doctor finished second 2m 23s ahead of the Gordini. A week later on the Reims circuit Jean Behra's Gordini actually beat Ascari and Farina in their Ferraris helped perhaps by Alberto having to stop at his pit with overheating. Unfortunately, for the Frenchman the race did not count for the world championship as the 'Automobile Club de France' had chosen the Rouen circuit in Normandy to host its Grand Prix.

• **84**_ Rouen-les-Essarts 6th July 1952: Ascari in the "Nouveau Monde" hairpin is about to lap Swiss privateer Rudi Fischer in his 12-cylinder F2 Ferrari.

6th July 1952: ACF Grand Prix. Rouen-les-Essarts, 3 hours (77 laps of the 5.020 kms circuit: 386.874 kms). Twenty cars started including an A6GCM Maserati originally destined for Fangio and entrusted to French veteran Philippe Etancelin. In 1952, drivers were forced to wear a proper helmet for international events which was not at all to the old Norman's liking whose favourite headgear was his famous cap turned back to front. The organisers finally waived the strict application of the rule and allowed him to wear a cycling helmet! Ascari, Farina and their fellow drivers had all given up linen helmets and Alberto sported a hard helmet painted blue his favourite colour. Like Fangio he often raced in a T-shirt. Driving suits were only used when it rained. Also entered were a couple of modified Ecurie Platé 4-cylinder Maseratis for Franco-American Harry Schell and Swiss Emmanuel de Graffenried. Yves Giraud-Cabantous joined the HWM regulars Collins and Macklin while Mike Hawthorn drove a singleton Cooper-Bristol.

In practice Ascari again set pole in 2m 14.8s ahead of Farina in 2m 16.2s and Taruffi in 2m 17.2s. Behra and Manzon in their 2-litres Gordinis made up the second row in 2m 19.3s and 2m 20.4s respectively. The start was given in front of some 80,000 spectators massed around the magnificent wooded circuit which provided them with excellent viewing especially in the mind-blowing descent to the "Nouveau Monde" hairpin. It had been raining and the track was still wet when Charles Faroux dropped the flag. Ascari jumped into the lead from Farina and the two Gordinis, which had passed Taruffi. On lap 3 Behra went off but managed to limp back to the Gordini

pit where his car was repaired and a wheel replaced. He charged back out and made a scintillating comeback to seventh place. It meant one rival less for the Ferraris. In fact, such was their domination that the race quickly turned into a rather boring procession as Ascari gradually opened up a lead over Farina: on lap 10 it was 11 seconds and after two hours' racing it was up to 1m 7s. He also broke the lap record on several occasions leaving it at 2m 17.3s a speed of 133.721 km/h.

When the rain began to fall again at half-distance the die had been cast and the Ferraris finished one, two, three with Alberto's win increasing his score in the world championship to eighteen points. He now led Taruffi by 5 points and Farina by 6. Manzon was again the first of the non-Ferraris in fourth place.

19th July 1952: British Grand Prix at Silverstone. 85 laps of the 4.710 km circuit: 400.395 kms. Among the thirty-one cars at the start were the three works Ferraris plus four private entries, two works A6GCS Maseratis driven by Bianco and Cantoni plus the two Platé entries. There were also four Gordinis but no Behra as he had been injured in a race in Sables d'Olonne. English teams included four Alta-engined Connaughts making their debut in their home race, four HWMs, five Cooper-Bristols, a works Alta and Moss in his G-Type ERA. This time it was Farina on pole although Ascari had been credited with the same time (1m 50s) but later. In fact, timing to within 1/10th of a second did not appear at Silverstone until 1958! Completing the front row were Taruffi in 1m 53s and Manzon's Gordini in 1m 55s. Once again it was Ascari who jumped straight into the lead from Farina and he soon opened up a gap. The Gordinis hit

• **85_** Silverstone 19th July 1952: A magnificent profile shot of Ascari and his Ferrari in the British Grand Prix on his way to another win. His relaxed driving style is clearly shown.

• 86_ In the same race Ascari is about to lap Stirling Moss at the wheel of the G-Type ERA, which was a flop. It retired when its 6-cylinder Bristol engine overheated.

• 87_ Ascari takes the chequered flag and a well deserved victory; some consolation for his defeat the previous year. He also set fastest lap adding an extra point to his championship score.

mechanical problems early on and to the delight of the English crowd Poore and Downing in their Connaughts held off Taruffi's Ferrari until lap 14 when the Silver Fox got past and the Ferraris assumed their familiar one, two, three formation. By lap 20 Ascari already had 19 seconds in hand over Farina and they were both lapping in 1m 53s. Farina then had to stop for a plug change and when he rejoined he drove like a man possessed finishing sixth overall. Thus on lap 40 Ascari led Taruffi by 1m 47s and 1m 57s behind came Dennis Poore closely followed by Hawthorn's acrobatic Cooper-Bristol. So Ascari took another unchallenged win with a lap in hand over Taruffi setting fastest lap in 1m 52s as the race neared its end. Into third came Mike Hawthorn and his performance added to his brilliant drive into fourth in Belgium had caught Ugolini's eye. The young bow-tied Englishman would be incorporated into the Ferrari squad for the 1953 season.

3rd August 1952: German Grand Prix. 18 laps of the 22.813 km Nürburgring circuit: 410.580 kms. This time the field numbered thirty cars including the usual trio of works 500 F2s plus four 166 F2s in private hands, two A6GC Maseratis and a new A6GCM entrusted to Felice Bonetto, three Gordinis with Behra making his return plus a host of German single-seaters, AFMs, Veritas and BMW specials all of which were powered by 6-cylinder engines derived from the pre-war 328 BMW power unit with its hemispherical cylinder head. England was represented by three HWMs and the Aston-Butterworth but neither Connaught nor Cooper-Bristol turned up. Ascari set pole in 10m 4.9s which compared with his best the previous year in the 375 F1 of 9m 55.8s, was 9.1s slower: not such a huge gap given the difference in power compensated for by the nimble F2 500's handling. The start was given in dry conditions and once again Ascari made the best getaway with Manzon on his heels followed by Farina and Bonetto. But not for long as the impudent Frenchman was quickly overtaken by the doctor. Bonetto spun on the first lap involving both Trintignant's Gordini and Pietsch's Veritas-Meteor: all three retired. Ascari duly racked up his fourth straight win of the season despite a quick stop on lap 16 to top up his oil and set the fastest lap in 10m 5.1s a speed of 135.706 km/h. He was followed home by Farina. This victory brought his total of points in the championship to 36 double that of Farina in second place.

• **88**_ Ascari and Taruffi exchange smiles on the rostrum. The "Silver Fox" gave the F2 500 its first world championship win in the Swiss Grand Prix and on the Silverstone circuit he finished second.

• **89**_ Nürburgring 3rd August 1952: Another Ascari win plus a Ferrari double thanks to Farina. followed him home. By setting the fastest lap Ascari looked an odds-on favourite for the 1952 world championship title.

• **90**_ Ascari's smile is a bit forced while Dr. Farina looks exhausted. The 409.9 kms racing on the Nordschliefe was as tough a test for the drivers as for the cars.

● **91**_ Zandvoort 17ᵗʰ August 1952: Pole, victory and fastest lap, a hat trick for Ascari on the Dutch circuit laid out in the dunes. A tight grip on the steering wheel was necessary due to the violent gusts of wind sweeping in from the North Sea.

17ᵗʰ August 1952: Dutch Grand Prix.
90 laps of the 4.193 km Zandvoort circuit: 377.370 kms. This time there were only eighteen starters and in the Ferrari squad Villoresi replaced Taruffi. Stirling Moss was back for another try in the ERA-Bristol and also entered were Mike Hawthorn in his Cooper-Bristol, Ken Downing's Connaught and Ken Wharton in a single-seater Frazer-Nash. In practice Hawthorn upset the Ferrari applecart by outpacing Villoresi and put his Cooper-Bristol on the outside of the front row alongside Farina and Ascari in their 500s F2 with Alberto on pole. Mike's best was 1m 51s while the two Ferrari drivers got round in 1m 46.5s and 1m 48.6s respectively. Villoresi shared the second row in 1m 51.8s with Maurice Trintignant's Gordini who lapped in 1m 53s. The start was given in wet conditions and a cheeky Hawthorn shot past Farina to latch onto Ascari's tail. Not for long as Nino repassed the Englishman on lap 2 and on lap 4 Villoresi did the same. So the three red cars were back in their usual positions in front of the green Cooper-Bristol and a trio of blue Gordinis. As the rain intensified Ascari relentlessly increased his lead. With a third of the race gone he was 26 seconds ahead of Farina, over a minute at two-thirds distance despite a stop to change wheels. As the end approached the rain stopped and the track dried out he dialled in the quickest lap in 1m 49.8s, an average of 137.475 km/h racking up victory number five ahead of Farina and

Villoresi while Hawthorn's fourth place confirmed his seat in the Maranello squad for the following season. Alberto now had 45 points as compared to Farina's 24 and was virtually assured of the world championship title even if he had to start subtracting points from his score.

7ᵗʰ September 1952: Italian Grand Prix.
80 laps of the 6.300 km circuit: 504 kms. Only twenty-four cars were allowed to start the Italian Grand Prix and they included no fewer than five works Ferraris in the hands of Ascari, Farina, Taruffi, Villoresi and Frenchman André Simon seen occasionally in Gordinis plus Louis Rosier and Swiss Rudi Fischer in their private 500s F2. There were six Maseratis, three A6GCMs for Gonzalez, making a comeback, Bonetto and Rol plus three A6GCs for Bianco, Landi and Cantoni. Frenchman Elie Bayol drove his OCSA. Connaught entered three cars for Poore, Ken McAlpine (one of the company sharholders) and Stirling Moss who had had enough of the ERA. Spearheading the Cooper-Bristol attack was Mike Hawthorn and backing him up were Ken Wharton, Alan Brown and Eric Brandon. The cars lined up four by four with Ascari (who else?) on pole in 2m 5.7s ahead of Villoresi and Farina and joining them on the front row was Maurice Trintignant in his Gordini who set an excellent fourth quickest time in 2m 7.2s. On row 2 were Gonzalez's Maserati, Taruffi's Ferrari, Manzon's Gordini and Simon in the last of the works

500s F2. Hawthorn and Moss were both on the third row. Juan Manuel Fangio, still recovering from his injuries, gave the start. In the lead at the end of lap 1 was Gonzalez as the tubby Argentinian had started with a half-full tank, followed by Trintignant and Ascari with Villoresi and Manzon on his heels. Alberto got past the Gordini on lap 3 but already Gonzalez had opened up a gap of seven seconds. On lap 5 Trintignant's brilliant drive came to a premature halt when his valve gear broke so the positions were: Gonzalez, Ascari, Villoresi, Bonetto's Maserati and Farina. For the first time that year the Scuderia was not having things all its own way. Then on lap 37 the leading Maserati shot into the pits for fuel and rear tyres while the Ferraris had planed to cover the whole distance (one of the longest of the season) without refuelling. He rejoined in fifth place over a minute behind. By half-distance he had passed

Bonetto and then he set about the Ferraris, his tubby frame quivering with the excitement of battle. He slashed past Farina and began to pull in Villoresi. Ascari then upped the pace and set the fastest lap in 2m 6.3s which Gonzalez bested with 2m 6.1s, a time that Alberto equalled in turn thus they shared the one point awarded for the quickest lap. On Lap 62 Villoresi was obliged to stop briefly and Gonzalez hurtled by to take second. But he could do nothing about Ascari who took the chequered flag to win his first world championship. His record read: six Grands Prix (excluding Indianapolis), six victories, six fastest laps. While he had the best car as the 500 F2 had no real rivals despite Gonzalez's brave efforts and occasional flashes from the Gordinis, his was a mind-blowing performance and he completely dominated his team-mates. Aged 34 he was on his way to becoming part of F1 legend after Farina and Fangio. ■

• **92**_ Monza 7th September 1952: Alberto notched up his sixth consecutive win in the Italian Grand Prix and with it his first world championship title in front of his home crowd. The photographers of those days were a fearless (rash?) bunch!

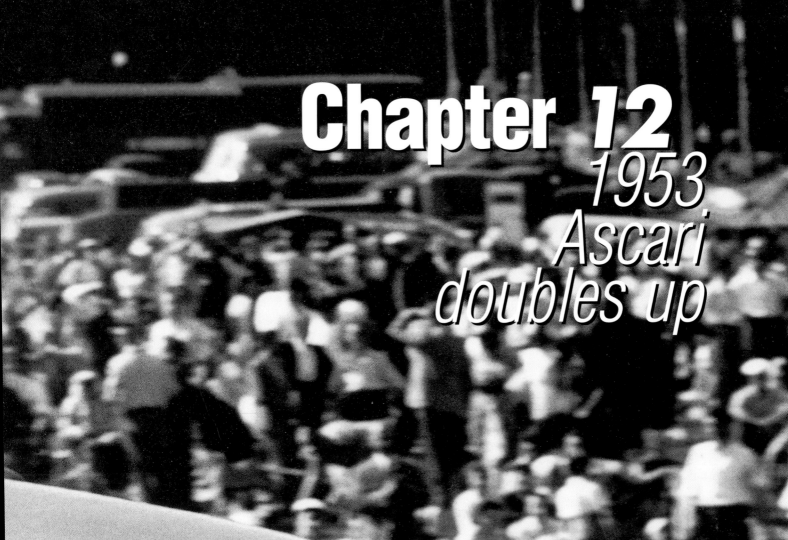

Chapter 12
1953
Ascari
doubles up

18th January 1953: Ascari won
the first Argentinian Grand Prix
counting for the world
championship, which was
overshadowed by a tragic
accident. *(Collection Maniago)*

18th January 1953: Argentinian Grand Prix. 96 laps of the 4.02 km Autodromo 17th October Buenos Aires: 385.920 kms. To counter the Maserati threat looming on the horizon Lampredi had worked his magic on the Ferrari engine during the winter: it now had 180 bhp to power the 600 kg 500 F2 which was 20 kilos more than the A6GCM Maserati but the latter used more fuel. Enzo again put his trust in Ascari, Villoresi and Farina joined by young English coming-man Mike Hawthorn. The Maserati line-up consisted of Fangio, making his comeback, Gonzalez, Oscar Galvez and Felice Bonetto. The Argentinian Grand Prix was on the world championship calendar for the first time and the ambience surrounding it was frenzied to say the least. General Peron used it to inaugurate a new ultra-modern circuit complex some 40 kms outside Buenos Aires which was invaded by over 400,000 excited spectators. In a misplaced "democratic" gesture to the crowd Peron ordered

the police to lower the safety barriers shortly before the start of the race; an act that was to have tragic consequences.
Ascari, who had walked the circuit, set pole in 1m 55.4s while alongside him was Fangio's Maserati in 1m 56.1s ahead of Farina's Ferrari. When the flag fell the Maranello no.1 made his usual lightning getaway and at the end of the first lap was in front of Farina and Fangio. Tragedy struck on lap 32 when Farina went off avoiding a child crossing the track. His Ferrari ploughed into the spectators killing nine and injuring forty. There was worse to come as an ambulance rushing to the scene of the accident also went into the crowd increasing the death toll and confusion. The race was NOT stopped and the drivers continued as best they could. Fangio was the only one able to pressure Ascari but went out on lap 36 with universal joint failure. Ascari strolled home to a hollow victory setting fastest lap followed by Villoresi, Gonzalez and Hawthorn.

• **95_** Zandvoort 7th June 1953: Ascari, Fangio, Farina are all smiles at Gigi Villoresi's attempt at a bit of "Comedia del Arte." Alberto won from Farina while Villoresi set the fastest lap.

• **96_** Le Mans 13th June 1953: A pit stop for the 375 MM Ferrari driven by Ascari-Villoresi. It posed the principal threat to the winning C-Type Jaguars for a long time until the Italians retired with a broken clutch.

7th June 1953 : Dutch Grand Prix.

90 laps of the 4.185 km Zandvoort circuit: 376.650 kms. The Dutch circuit had been slightly modified and the kerbing partly redone. As always the sand and wind represented the principal risk factors for the drivers. Ascari set pole in 1m 51.1s while Fangio again split the Ferraris with the second-quickest lap ahead of Farina. In the race Alberto vanished into the sunset as was his wont and both Villoresi and Farina got past Fangio. The Maserati was never a threat and the ex-world champion retired on lap 37 with transmission problems. Gonzalez, who had made a dreadful start, provided the main interest in the race as he fought his way up to third place taking over Bonetto's Maserati when his own went out with a rear axle problem on lap 23. Ascari scored an unchallenged victory but for once fastest lap eluded him as this honour fell to Villoresi.

• **97**_ Spa-Francorchamps
21st June 1953: Ascari takes
the chequered flag. For once
he did not have things all his
own way in his 500 F2 Ferrari
as the Maseratis driven by
Fangio and Gonzalez were
quicker in the opening stages
with Froilan setting the fastest
lap. Reliability, though, was
not their strong point.

21st June 1953 : Belgian Grand Prix.

36 laps of the 14.080 km circuit: 506.880 kms. This was the race where the Maseratis finally showed they were capable of toppling Ferrari. Fangio set pole in 4m 30s two seconds quicker than Ascari who found himself the meat in a Modena sandwich as Gonzalez put his A6GCM on the outside of the front row. The performance of the Trident-badged cars renewed interest in a championship that had fallen into a state of somnolence such was Ferrari's domination. And it was not Ascari who shot into the lead at flag fall but Gonzalez hotly pursued by Fangio. The two Argentineans waged a titanic battle for the lead in the opening laps while Ascari sat back awaiting developments and let them get on with it,. These were not long in coming as on lap 12 Gonzalez broke his accelerator and one lap later Fangio's engine expired. And so Ascari found himself back in his usual position followed by Hawthorn, Farina and Villoresi. Gigi soon came under threat from Onofre Marimon making his debut in the Maserati team and was obliged to cede fourth to the young Argentinian. Fangio in the meantime had taken over Johnny Claes's car and was blasting his way back up the field. He overtook de Graffenried and Trintignant locked in battle for fifth and taking advantage of Hawthorn's and Farina's mechanical problems got up to third. However, he overdid it in the final lap and went off at Stavelot, fortunately without serious injury. Ascari duly notched up the last of his nine consecutive victories from Luigi Villoresi and Marimon while fastest lap fell to Gonzalez.

● **98_** Reims 7th July 1953: Ascari again set pole for the ACF Grand Prix but was unable to match the pace of his young English team-mate Mike Hawthorn (n°.16) in the race. The latter fought a duel with Fangio's Maserati (n°.18) that has become part of motor racing myth. Alberto finished fourth only 4.6 seconds behind the winner!

• **99_** Silverstone 18th July: Is a slightly worried Alberto asking himself whether or not the young blond Brit with the bow tie is going to repeat his French success in front of his home crowd?

• **100_** Starting from pole Ascari dominated the race and scored another win on the Silverstone circuit even if he had to share fastest lap with Gonzalez in his Maserati.

Ascari was to taste defeat on the Reims circuit in the French Grand Prix, one of the few races in which he did not dominate his rivals during the 1952-53 seasons. On 5th July in the searing heat of the champagne region he let his young team-mate Mike Hawthorn set off in hot pursuit of Fangio's Maserati whom he beat in one of the greatest races in the history of the sport. Ascari was not even in the top three as Gonzalez in his Maserati nicked third from the Italian in the closing minutes of the race. Only 4.6 seconds covered the first four! In Great Britain Ascari was back on the topmost step of the rostrum ahead of Fangio. In the German round he set pole in

9m 59.8s the first driver to dip under the 10-minute barrier in an F2 car. He held onto the lead until on lap 5 when the left-hand front

Mike Hawthorn:
"Ascari was determined to get ahead"

"Ascari, who was always brilliant on this terribly difficult 14,5 miles mountain and forest circuit, had made fastest practice lap, Fangio led at the start, with Ascari and myself right on his tail. Ascari was determined to get ahead and during the first few miles he nearly rammed Fangio as he braked for the corners with smoke pouring from the car. He managed it and had a useful lead by the end of the first lap, leaving Fangio and I to fight it out once more. I passed him in front of the grandstand, but he got past again and we went on passing and re-passing right round the course. At five laps I spotted Ascari at the pits and there seemed to be a certain amount of excitement, but I only learned afterwards what a narrow escape from disaster he had had, right in front of the grandstand. Coming up towards the pits on a part of the course which is fortunately fairly straight, he had lost a front wheel at about 140 mph and saw it go bounding away into the blue. He managed to hold the car straight and went screeching past the pits on three wheels and a brake drum. I think it was due to a hub nut coming loose. A mechanic ran after him with a jack and another wheel was fitted, but the braking was uneven after that and Ascari soon took over Villoresi's car; he set up a new lap record in 9'56" and was catching me up very rapidly indeed when the engine disintegrated."

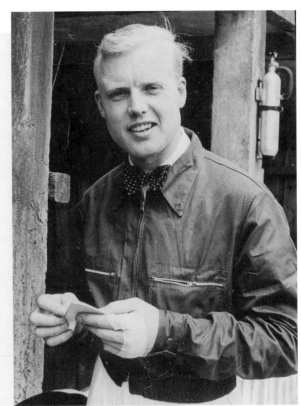

• **102_** A cool Ascari laps Lance Macklin's HWM in Stowe corner, which later retired with clutch problems. Alberto went on to win by a minute from Fangio's Maserati.

• **103_** Nürburgring
2nd August 1953: Fangio in his
Maserati (n°.5) makes the best
getaway at the start of the
German Grand Prix from the
Ferraris of Hawthorn (n°.3),
Farina (n°.2) and Ascari
(n°.1). A little further back are
Trintignant in his Gordini
(n°.10) and Villoresi in the last
of the works 500s F2 (n°.4).

• **104_** On lap 5 of the
German Grand Prix Ascari's
Ferrari shed its right-hand
front wheel. He somehow
managed to keep it on the
track and limped two
kilometres to his pit on the
brake drum.
(Barth Völker archives)

• **105_** He was unable to brake
early enough to stop at his pit so his
car was pushed back on a jack by
two mechanics as allowed by the
regulations. He restarted and got
back up to fifth place.
(Barth Völker archives)

• **106_** He then took over Villoresi's car (n°. 4) in which he set the fastest lap while fighting his way back to fourth place until the engine let go due to an oil leak. Victory finally went to Farina from Fangio's Maserati.
(Barth Völker archives)

• **107_** After his second retirement Ascari (seen from behind with hand luggage and helmet box) stomped off in his suit and tie. That day Dame Fortune did not smile on him but he was still well in the lead in the world championship with 33.5 points as against Fangio's 19.

• **108_** Ascari met Tazio
Nuvolari on several occasions
(here in the Modena Grand Prix
paddock). Il campionissimo
held Alberto in high esteem and
considered him as his natural
successor. Tazio died in his bed
in his Mantua home on
11ᵗʰ August 1953 and was
mourned by the whole Italian
nation. It was the end of an era
in motor racing.
(DR)

• **109_** Berne-Bremgarten
20ᵗʰ August 1953: the start of the
Swiss Grand Prix. Fangio waits
impassively and Ascari in the
middle of the front row glances
at his nearest rival while a
frantic mechanic tries to start Farina's
Ferrari. The Ferrari triple with
Ascari leading home Farina and
Hawthorn was a fitting tribute to
the great Nuvolari. Alberto also
set the fastest lap and wrapped
up his second world
championship title. Though no
one knew it at the time it was to
be the Italian's last world
championship victory.
(Maniago collection)

wheel of his Ferrari parted company with the hub. Ascari must have felt it coming (see Hawthorn's comments) as he managed to limp back to his pit. He took over Villoresi's car and finally finished in a lowly eight position although again retiring before the end. Victory went to Farina (his last in a World Championship Grand Prix) while Fangio finished in an impressive second place.

Less than two weeks after the German Grand Prix Tazio Nuvolari died on 11th August in Mantua plunging the whole of Italy into mourning. Then it was back to business again for Ascari with the Swiss Grand Prix on 22nd August. Fangio put his Maserati on pole but was unable to prevent the current world champion from opening up a big lead. With two-thirds of the race gone Alberto was obliged to pit to change plugs as his engine was missing. Giving the lie to those who said that he was incapable of driving a really competitive race if he was not in first place he made an awesome comeback setting fastest lap and passing Marimon, Farina and Hawthorn to retake the lead. Fangio had run into mechanical problems forcing him to take over Bonetto's Maserati in which he came home fourth. Ascari's victory assured him of his second consecutive world championship title.

• **110**_ Nürburgring 30th August 1953: Ferrari entered a 375 MM Viginale-bodied open 2-seater for Ascari and Farina (seen here refuelling) in the Nürburging 1000 kms race. They won the event giving the Scuderia another 8 points towards the Sport Car World Championship for Makes. (Barth Völker archives)

• **111_** Monza
13th September 1953: Lap after lap the battle raged between Fangio's and Marimon's Maseratis (n° 50 and 54) and the Ferraris driven by Ascari (n°.4) and Farina (n°.6) to the delight of the spectators.

The final round of the world championship was at Monza on 13th September and was one of the most closely-fought races in the history of F1 thanks to an epic battle between Ascari and Farina and Fangio and Marimon, two Ferraris versus two Maseratis. Lap after lap these four swapped places until Marimon was obliged to stop at his pit on lap 46 to plug a leak in his radiator and rejoined right in the midst of the battling trio. The cars passed and repassed each other with the suspense building up as the last turn on the final lap approached. But right on the racing line was a slower car, McAlpine's Connaught. Ascari made a split-second decision to go round him on the outside, lost control of his Ferrari which went broadside and was hit by Marimon's Maserati. Farina took to the grass to avoid them while Fangio nipped though on the inside to take the chequered flag from a rather surprised Villoresi. Alberto, who was a very superstitious man, later remarked that it was the thirteenth! He was slightly injured but was able to walk back to the pits with Marimon after which he went up on the rostrum to congratulate Fangio.

Although beaten in front of his home crowd Alberto had the satisfaction of becoming the first ever Formula 1 double world champion, his final score being 34.5 points. Fangio was second with 28 and Farina third with 26. In his F2 Ferrari Ascari also won the Syracuse, Pau, Marseille, Comminges, and La Baule Grands Prix in 1952 and Pau again plus Bordeaux in 1953. The same year he came first in the Nürburgring 1000 kms in a 375 MM Ferrari with Farina in which they beat the three works D 24 Lancias in the hands of Fangio-Bonetto, Taruffi-Manzon and Castellotti-Bracco despite suspension problems. On 31st May he scored a victory in the Formula Libre event on the Albi circuit in his 375 F1 after a fabulous battle with Fangio's V16 BRM. In the Le Mans 24 Hours race the same year Ascari and Villoresi in their 375 MM coupe gave the works C-Type Jaguars a good run for their money until retiring in the nineteenth hour. Finally, together with Villoresi he helped Ferrari to another double in the Casablanca 12 Hours race behind Farina. A fresh challenge beckoned as the 1954 season approached. ∎

• **112_** Ascari is just in front of Fangio and is hoping to make it a hat trick on the Monza circuit after his wins in 1951 and 1952. It was not to be.

• **113_** When Ascari went broadside trying to avoid a tail-ender Marimon could not avoid hitting him. Alberto looks furious while the young Argentinian tries to explain the incident to an official.

• **114_** The 1954 Mille
Miglia saw Ascari in his D 24
Lancia beat the Ferrari armada
after a brilliant drive. It was a
just revenge for his mishap
three years previously and
some compensation for a very
frustrating F1 season.

Chapter 13
1954-1955
A new challenge

The new F1 regulations announced by the CSI
two years previously came into force in
1954. Maximum cubic capacity for
unsupercharged engines was 2500 ccs and for
supercharged ones 750 ccs. There was no weight
limit. The Ferrari engineers were working on two
new cars, the 625 powered by a 4-cylinder engine
derived from the 500 F2 and the 555 nicknamed
the "Squalo." The 625 had a 2498 cc power unit
obtained by increasing the bore and stroke (94 x
90 mm) which put out 250 bhp at 7200 rpm
while the "Squalo" was powered by a 2497.5 cc
(100 x 79.5) 4-cylinder engine with two valves
per cylinder which also developed 250 bhp at
7500 rpm. It had a new chassis and being 10
kilometres lighter should have been quicker than
the 625. The 1954 Ferrari drivers were Farina,
Trintignant, Gonzalez, Hawthorn and occasionally
Manzon.

Maserati was busy with the first prototype
of the 250F whose straight 6 engine was derived
from the final evolution of the F2 A6GCM
sometimes designated the A6SS/G whose
performance had improved by leaps and bounds

during the 1953 season. The 2.5 litres version put
out 240 bhp initially and the works cars were
driven by Fangio, Marimon, Mantovani, Musso
and Bira while Stirling Moss campaigned his as a
privateer. Amédée Gordini, financially
embarrassed as always, enlarged his 2-litres
engine to 2.5 litres, which gave the cars some
220 bhp. They were entrusted to Behra, Simon,
Bayol and Belgian Andre Pilette.

However, the little world of Formula 1 was
agog with excitement at the imminent return of
Mercedes-Benz to Grand Prix racing. In Stuttgart,
the engineers Uhlenhaut, Scherenberg and
Nallinger, who looked after the design office of
the competitions service of the German company,
had considerable technical and financial means at
their disposal. They were working on a light alloy
straight eight engine with a desmodromic valve
gear system which put out around 280 bhp and
was housed in a streamlined bodywork. The
legendary Alfred Neubauer made a comeback as
team manager, a role that had made him famous
in the thirties. It all sounded very ominous for its
rivals but at least the cars would not be ready

Luigi Villoresi:
"If Alberto hadn't died...."

Gigi Villoresi, who died in 2001, was very closely linked to Ascari's life and career. In 1992 he recalled this era for the magazine "Auto Passion" and shared some of his memories with us:

"Ascari, Farina and myself got on very well at Ferrari. And Enzo didn't like that. His motto was 'Divide and rule!' We always agreed with each other. I drove for Ferrari until 1953 and then in October Ascari and I went to Maranello to renew our contracts. I said to Alberto,'I won't resign unless you do.' Then I spoke to Ungolini who told me, 'You're right Villoresi, we haven't treated you very well but from now on it'll be better; you'll have the best car,' and so on. 'OK,' I answered ,'but I won't sign if Alberto's not with me.' The latter had come to Modena but he already had a contract drawn up with Lancia. So we said to Ferrari, "Bye, bye see you again sometime!' Alberto showed me his contract with Lancia and said, 'Gigi, if you agree we'll both sign.' So we spent a year racing with Lancia. The car was fantastic but it was behind schedule and we had problems with the brakes and tyres.....

For me Ascari was one of the greatest. He'd won two world championships and I'm sure that if he hadn't been killed he'd have won several more. One day during a reception in Termo, Fangio – a great driver – was named honorary citizen of that town as his parents had had land there. There were three hundred guests and after dinner various drivers took the microphone to say a few words and answer questions from the floor. They spoke about everybody, Stirling Moss, Gonzalez, everybody except Ascari. It cut me to the quick. So when it was Fangio's turn, I said, 'do you mind,' and asked,: 'Fangio if Alberto hadn't been killed do you think you'd have won five world championships?' He replied very cleverly: 'Ah, when Alberto went into the lead, there was nothing you could do about it!' Of course, he couldn't have answered yes or no."

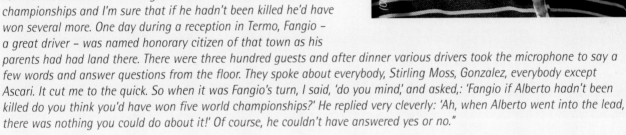

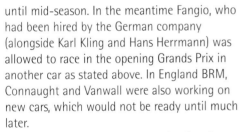

(Christian Bedei archives)

until mid-season. In the meantime Fangio, who had been hired by the German company (alongside Karl Kling and Hans Herrmann) was allowed to race in the opening Grands Prix in another car as stated above. In England BRM, Connaught and Vanwall were also working on new cars, which would not be ready until much later.

In Italy all eyes were turned to Lancia where a new F1 contender was being built. It was designated the D50 and was penned by legendary wizard Vittorio Jano. It contained technical solutions that were more audacious than those integrated into the Mercedes-Benz and of course, the same Jano had designed the P2 Alfa Romeo driven by Alberto's father, Antonio. Ascari was very interested in the technical characteristics of the D50. Its 90° V8 engine was a structural part of the short wheelbase chassis and was slightly offset to enable the drive shaft to pass alongside the driver which gave him a lower seating position thus lowering the centre of gravity of the car. At the rear was a final drive/gearbox unit and the

whole was enclosed in bodywork with side-mounted fuel tanks. The D50's engine put out 260 bhp and the car weighed 630 kgs like the Maserati as compared to the Gordinis and Ferrais which topped the scales at between 590 and 600 kgs while the Mercedes-Benz was the heaviest of the lot with 720 kilos

Lancia like Ferrari and Maserati had also mounted an attack on the Sports Car World Championship in which Ascari drove attracted by the dosh. Neither he nor Villoresi had obtained substantial salary increases or firm undertakings from Enzo Ferrari for their participation in sports car events. Indeed, during a meeting in Maranello on 29th December 1953 'il commendatore' had not unveiled his 1954 programme to the press and hinted at the fact that he was about to stop everything and entrust his cars to private teams as he did not have enough money to carry on. He even asked Ascari on the spot if he was ready to sign a contract for the whole of the 1954 season. The latter under contract until April 1954, refused. The next day he set out for Turin together with Villoresi.

• **117**_ Brescia 1st May
1954: A smiling Ascari about
to zoom off down the ramp and
tackle the Mille Miglia's
1660 kms over open roads.

Gianni Lancia was ready to offer his drivers a lot more money than Ferrari. In Ascari's case 25 million lira a year two-and-a-half times what he had been earning at Ferrari in 1953. So he jumped at the offer. In addition, he had a Lancia Aurelia B 20 GT as company car. The young and talented Eugenio Castellotti completed the line-up. Neither Lancia, nor Jano nor their drivers realised that they were about to tackle a season, which would be marked by delays. Ascari's first taste of a Lancia was a few laps in one of the D 24s for the forthcoming Sebring event. Then he did some shakedown tests of the D 50 on the Caselle airfield adjacent to Turin. Unfortunately the whole single-seater programme fell way behind schedule as there were a large number of problems to be ironed out with both the chassis and road-holding and the result was that the team missed all but one of the 1954 Grands Prix. Fangio had already begun his conquest of the 1954 title with a win in the Argentinian round in his Maserati followed home by three Ferraris driven by Farina, Gonzalez and Trintignant. On the Pau circuit Behra brought his Gordini home in first place beating Trintignant's Ferrari to the delight of the partisan crowd.

Ascari was champing at the bit and as Villoresi was indisposed following an accident during testing for the Mille Miglia he accepted to drive in the event even though it was not included in his contract. In November 1953, the 3.1 litres version of the D 24 had won the Carrera Panamericana in Mexico and for 1954 the V6's cubic capacity had been increased to 3.3 litres (88 x 90 mm bore and stroke 3284 ccs) for a power output of 265 bhp. They all retired in Sebring. Four were entered for the Mille Miglia driven by Castellotti, Taruffi, Ascari and Valenzano and their main opposition consisted of four works Ferraris (two 4.9 litres 375 Pluses for Farina and Maglioli and a pair of 4.5 litres 375 MMs for Paolo Marzotto and Piero Scotti). Also entered were two 3-litres models one of which was driven by veteran Clemente Biondetti, record holder of the highest number of wins in the event (4), racing in the Mille Miglia for the last time, and a couple of Aston Martins entrusted to Reg Parnell and Peter Collins. The race was held in pouring rain. Shortly after the start Farina had a big off, hit a tree and broke his arm while Maglioli and Taruffi were locked in combat for the lead. Ascari, who started at 6h02, was now

• 118_ Alberto checks in at one of the time controls during the event, which he chose to drive alone.

third on the road and when he reached Ravenna he was up to second followed by Castellotti who had passed Maglioli, and the Marzotto brothers. That put three Lancias in the first three places ahead of three Ferraris. By Pescara Alberto had been overtaken by Castellotti and was 5m 49s behind Taruffi but had 42 seconds in hand over Maglioli. In Rome Castellotti went out with transmission problems and Ascari inherited second place again 4 minutes behind Taruffi. Shortly after leaving the Italian capital on the second leg of the race the leading Lancia went off while trying to overtake a tail-ender. Taruffi tried to repair his car and got going again only to retire for good in Florence. So Ascari was now in the lead but all was not well with his car, which was suffering from problems with its accelerator and oil tank. The gap between him and Marzotto was 5m 59s with Maglioli a further five seconds back. Alberto was not very keen on continuing and considered retiring but he was persuaded to try and reach Bologna where Lancia had a service crew waiting. Both Ferraris went out, Marzotto because of a broken gearbox while Maglioli crashed, luckily

without injury. In Bologna such was Ascari's lead over his closest pursuer (Marzotto's 2-litres Ferrari Mondial) that he was able to have the split oil tank repaired and the accelerator spring replaced. He restarted carefully and saluted as he passed the Mantua graveyard wherein Nuvolari reposed. He then upped the pace covering the final section Cremona-Mantua-Brescia at a record speed for which he was awarded the first "Trofeo Nuvolari" and arrived victorious in Brescia having averaged 139.645 km/h with more than 34 minutes in hand over the runner up. Lancia's win in the Mille Miglia put an end to six years of Ferrari domination.

The make did not compete in the Le Mans 24 Hours race, which Ferrari won. In fact, three D 24s were entered for Ascari-Villoresi, Fangio-Taruffi and Manzon-Castellotti but they were withdrawn by Gianni Lancia. What was more worrying was the fact that the D 50 F1 programme was falling even further behind schedule. There was no Belgian Grand Prix for Ascari, Villoresi and Castellotti where Fangio added another nine points to his championship tally thanks to a win and fastest lap. Then came the French Grand Prix on 4th July and the long-

awaited debut of the W 196 Mercedes-Benz in the hands of Fangio, Kling and Herrmann. Gianni Lancia, however, managed to negotiate the loan of a brace of works 250 F Maseratis for Ascari and Villoresi. Fangio set pole on the Reims circuit in 2m 29.4s ahead of Kling in 2m 30.4s. However, Ascari showed that he had lost none of his fire by putting his Maserati on the outside of the front row with a lap in 2m 30.5s. Then as the cars flashed past the pits at the end of lap 1 Kling led from Fangio, Gonzalez's Ferrari and Alberto's Maserati. However it was all too much for the 250 F and on the following lap the transmission went. When Gonzalez's Ferrari's engine blew on lap 12 the way was clear for the German cars to score a double on their first outing with Fangio winning from Kling. Villoresi managed to bring his Maserati home in fifth place.

As the D 50s were still not ready (Ascari had crashed one at Monza just a week before the

British Grand Prix) Maserati again lent two 250 Fs to Ascari and Villoresi for the English event at Silverstone on 17th July. Victory went to Gonzalez (author of the second quickest time in practice) in his Ferrari who dominated the race as he had done three years earlier. Fangio was not as fast as expected. His Mercedes' streamlining hindered his vision on a circuit whose limits were defined by sand-filled oilcans and in addition he lost fourth then third gear! In addition, the Continental tyres on the German cars proved less effective in the wet than the Pirellis. All three works Maseratis started from the back of the grid as they arrived too late for official practice. Ascari fought his way up to sixth place and was then forced to stop on lap 9 with steering problems. He rejoined but retired on lap 21 with a dropped valve. He took over Villoresi's car, which went out with a broken connecting rod on lap 41. Marimon's Maserati finished third behind Hawthorn and Gonzalez and ahead of Fangio.

1954 ACF Grand Prix
Maserati 250 F

P. MÉNARD

Designers : Gioacchino Colombo and Giulio Alfieri

Engine
Make/type: Maserati 250 F
No. of cylinders: straight 6 (front)
Cubic capacity: 2493.9 ccs
Bore and stroke: 84 x 75 mm
Compression ratio: 12:1
Max. power: 240 bhp
Max. revs: 7200 rpm
Block: light alloy
Carburettors: 3 double choke Webers
Distribution: D.O.H.C
No. of valves per cylinder: 2
Ignition: 2 magentos (Marelli)
No. of plugs per cylinder: 2

Transmission
Gearbox/no. of ratios: Maserati transversal/ 4+ reverse
Clutch: Maserati dry multiplate

Chassis
Type: tubular
Suspension: Twin rocker arms, front/de Dion rear with semi-elliptic springs/rear
Shock absorbers: telescopic, heliocoidal springs
Wheels: 5.50 x 16 (Front) / 7.00 x 16 (Rear)
Tyres: Pirelli
Brakes: drums on all 4 wheels

Dimensions
Wheelbase: 2280 mm
Tracks: 1300 mm (Front) / 1250 mm (Rear)
Fuel tank capacity: 200 litres
Dry weight: 620 kgs

Used in the 1954 ACF and British Grands Prix.

During the summer Ascari, Villoresi and a few other drivers found themselves in Monaco for the shooting of an American film called *"The Racers"* adapted from the novel by pre-war Swiss-German driver Hans Ruesch. They took part in the racing scenes that interspersed the love action between hero Kirk Douglas and heroine Bella Darvi. Ascari's next event was the Italian Grand Prix on 5th September as he did not take part in either the German or Swiss rounds (where Fangio clinched his second title). And to everybody's surprise he was in a Ferrari! The Scuderia entered six cars for Hawthorn, Trintignant, Gonzalez, Maglioli, Manzon and Ascari who was at the wheel of a 625 chassis with a new version of the 553 engine. In practice he hammered round the Monza circuit to set the second quickest time in 1m 59.2s beaten only by the inevitable Fangio in 1m 59s while third went to Moss in 1m 59.3s. Behind them on the second row were Kling's Mercedes-Benz, Gonzalez's

Ferrari and Villoresi's Maserati. It looked like being a pretty hectic start as the star drivers of all three makes were grouped in 1.2 seconds. Right from flag fall Kling and Fangio hit the front followed by Gonzalez, Ascari and Moss. On lap 2 the Pampas Bull moved up to third and Fangio was monstering Kling who made a mistake in Lesmo and dropped back to fifth. On lap 6 Ascari went into the lead to the delight of the crowd ahead of Gonzalez, Fangio and Moss. For the next 43 laps the battle raged between the two world champions with Moss on their heels, the Englishman even nipping past both to lead briefly. But for Ascari it all went wrong on lap 49 when a valve blew on his Ferrari. Moss then took over the lead and looked set to win until an oil leak brought his race to a halt on lap 69. And so Fangio went on to score a slightly unexpected victory as both the Ferrari and the Maserati had out-paced him.

1954 Italian Grand Prix
Ferrari 625 F1

P. MÉNARD

Designer : Aurelio Lampredi

Engine

Make/type: Ferrari/625
No. of cylinders: straight 4 (front)
Cubic capacity: 2498.3 ccs
Bore & stroke: 94 x 90 mm
Compression ratio: 13:1
Max. power: 250 bhp
Max. revs: 7200 rpm
Block: alloy/steel liners
Carburettors: 2 50 DCOA Webers
Distribution: D.O.H.C
No. of valves per cylinder: 2
Ignition: 2 magnetos
No. of plugs per cylinder: 2

Transmission

Gearbox/ no. of speeds: Ferrari longitudinal/4 + reverse
Clutch: multiplate

Chassis

Type: steel tubing
Suspension: double wishbone, lower transversal leaf springs,
front/deDion tube, longitudinal push rods, lower transversal leaf
springs/rear
Shock absorbers: Houdaille vane type
Wheels: spoked Borranis
Tyres: 5.50 x 16 (Front) / 7.00 x 16 (Rear) Englebert
Brakes: drums on all 4 wheels

Dimensions

Wheelbase: 2160 mm
Tracks: 1278 mm (Front) / 1250 mm (Rear)
Fuel tank capacity: 180 litres
Dry weight: 600 kgs

Used in Italy in 1954.

• **120_** Monza 5ᵗʰ September 1954: Following forced withdrawals in Germany and Switzerland as the Lancia was still not ready, Ascari could not miss his home Grand Prix. He drove an F1 625 Ferrari on a one-off basis and performed miracles with it, as he was able to match the pace of both Fangio's Mercedes and Moss's Maserati until the engine cried enough. (Maniago collection)

• **121_** Dundrod 11th September 1954: The start of the Tourist Trophy on the narrow dangerous Dundrod circuit outside Belfast in Northern Ireland. The fantastic entry included Ascari in the n°.1 D 25 Lancia who jumps into the lead from the Rolt-Hamilton Jaguar n°.5.and behind them come the rest of the pack including the Swaters-Laurent C-Type Jaguar n°.11, the Abecassis-Meyer HWM-Jaguar n°.9, Fangio's works Lancia n°.2, Peter Collins's Aston Martin n°.18, the Gaze-Risely-Pritchard HWM-Jaguar n°.8, Castellotti's D 24 Lancia n°.4, Mike Hawthorn's Monza Ferrari n°.15 and the Flynn-Large C-Type Jaguar n°.10.

• **122_** Ascari went into an early lead until overtaken by Hawthorn. The differential broke on his Lancia and he retired.

• **123_** Ascari explains to Stirling Moss what happened in the hairpin.

133

• **124_** Monza October 1954: Ascari tests the D 50 Lancia in preparation for the Spanish Grand Prix.
(Maniago collection)

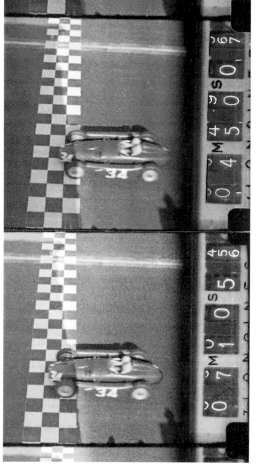

• **125_** Barcelona 24th October 1954: At long last the D 50 Lancias appeared for a race. These photos of the Spanish Grand Prix are taken from Longine's timing shots. Ascari set the fastest lap and led the race early on. His clutch went on the blink on lap 9 and he retired on lap 11.
(Maniago collection)

In September Ascari and Villoresi shared one of the three new 3.7 litres D25 Lancia sports cars entered for the Tourist Trophy on the Dundrod circuit in Northern Ireland. Early on Alberto was in the lead before being overtaken by the 750 Monza Ferrari in the hands of Hawthorn-Maglioli. He then handed over to Villoresi and when he got back behind the wheel for his next stint he was the victim of a broken propeller shaft.

On 24th October the Lancias finally appeared at a Grand Prix, the Spanish event on the Barcelona-Pedrables circuit. Two cherry red D50s were entered for Ascari and Villoresi after successful tests on the Caselle aerodrome, at San Remo and on the Monza circuit. Ascari put the Lancia on pole on its racing debut with a lap in 2m 18.5s. Second quickest was Fangio in 2m 19.1s and then came Hawthorn in 2m 20.6s and Harry Schell with a lap in 2m 20.6s. Lancia, Mercedes-Benz, Ferrari and Maserati made up the front row while Villoresi in the second D 50 was fifth in 2m 21s ahead of Moss and Musso's Maseratis.

When the flag fell in torrid conditions Harry Schell catapulted to the front ahead of Hawthorn, Ascari, Fangio and Herrmann. On lap 2 Villoresi coasted to a halt with a broken crankshaft bearing while Ascari had just

• **126_** Buenos Aires 16ᵗʰ January 1955: The Lancia mechanics push Ascari's and Villoresi's D 50s accompanied by their drivers to the grid for the Argentinian Grand Prix. *(Maniago collection)*

overtaken Hawthorn. Next time round he shot past Schell to put the Lancia into first place and began to pull away from his pursuers. Alas, on lap 9 he came into his pit with clutch problems and after a further exploratory lap the car was pushed away. However, he had the satisfaction of setting the fastest lap. Victory went to Mike Hawthorn, which was some consolation for Ferrari in what had been a pretty disappointing season after the halcyon years of 1952-53.

Jano and his team worked flat out in Turin during the winter to make the D 50 not only a fast car but also a reliable one capable of beating the Mercedes-Benz. On 16ᵗʰ January 1955 there were three D 50s in Argentina for the opening round of the world championship driven by Ascari, Villoresi and young Italian hope Eugenio Castellotti. Inspired by his home crowd Gonzalez put his Ferrari on pole in 1m 43.1s with Ascari 1/10s behind and sharing the front row with them were Fangio and Behra: Ferrari, Lancia, Mercedes and Maserati. The start was given in suffocating heat and Fangio got the drop on Gonzalez and Ascari. These three were quickly locked in battle and pulled away from the rest of the field. Already Lancia's challenge was blunted, as Villoresi retired on lap 2 with carburettor problems. He took over from Castellotti on lap 15. Ascari went to the front on lap 3 hotly pursued

by the two Argentineans. The fact that he managed to stay in the lead despite intense pressure in a car with erratic road holding was further proof of his exceptional skills. On lap 22, however, the Lancia got away from him and he spun off into the fencing damaging the D 50 enough to have to retire. Finally, Fangio won the race displaying remarkable endurance in the searing hot conditions.

• **127_** In the early stages of the race Ascari fought for the lead with Gonzalez's Ferrari (n°.12) but went off on lap 22 damaging the car too badly to continue. *(Maniago collection)*

When the cars arrived back in Turin Jano and his men got down to further improving their performance. In particular, the drivers insisted that he modify the braking system. The D 50 Lancias were then entered for three non-championship races in order to test their reliability before the Monaco Grand Prix. In Valentino Park in Turin on 27th March Ascari saw off his main rival Behra's Maserati and then took the lead which he held to the flag while Villoresi and Castellotti came home third and fourth respectively behind Roberto Mieres' Maserati but ahead of Harry Schell's

Ferrari. Although it was not a championship race and there were no Mercedes-Benz both Ferrari (Trintignant and Farina) and Maserati (Behra, Musso and Perdisa) had sent works cars so the Lancias' performance was very encouraging as all three finished. It was the same story in the Naples Grand Prix on 8th May on the 4.100 km Posillipo circuit (60 laps, 246 kms) with Ascari scoring another win after starting from pole. Villoresi finished third behind Musso's Maserati with Behra in fourth place. The Frenchman set the fastest lap in both events. Lancia sent three cars to Pau for

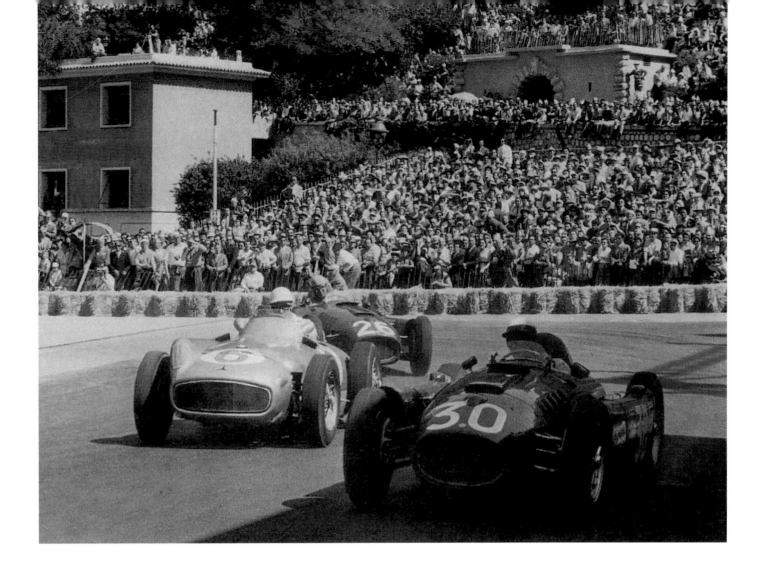

the annual Grand Prix held on 11th April over 110 laps, a distance of 304 kms. The circuit was laid out in the streets of Beaumont Park and put braking and accelerating to a severe test. Ascari had already won this event twice in an F2 Ferrari 500 but he was not destined to notch up a third success. He was on pole and had built up a good lead when he had to stop at his pit to repair a brake line, which cost him certain victory. He had to cover the last few laps with brakes on his front wheels only and finished fifth. Some consolation came in the form of fastest lap. First place went to Jean Behra in his Maserati giving him a double as he had won the race the year before in a Gordini. The other two Lancias made it to the finish with Castellotti in second place and Villoresi fourth. All in all it was a boost for the team's self-confidence as the Monaco and European Grand Prix approached.

On 22nd May as Mike Hawthorn later wrote there was a brilliant entry and a selection of champions almost unique in the history of F1 at the start of the Monaco event. The doyen was 56-year-old Louis Chiron who had been lent the fourth Lancia for what was to be his last Grand Prix (making him the oldest driver ever to race in a Grand Prix) and joining him on the grid were two 49-year-olds Giuseppe Farina and Piero Taruffi both in Ferraris plus the two double world

champions Ascari in his Lancia and Fangio in a Mercedes-Benz as well as 46-year-old Luigi Villoresi also Lancia-mounted. Louis Rosier, touching fifty entered his Maserati. The young guns were there too: 23-year-old Mike Hawthorn in a Vanwall, 25-year-old Stirling Moss in a Mercedes plus Italian coming man 25-year-old Eugenio Castellotti in another works Lancia and 30-year-old Luigi Musso in a Maserati. Frenchmen Jean Behra (Maserati) Maurice Trintignant (Ferrari) and Manzon, Bayol and Pollet in their Gordinis completed the line-up.

Mercedes-Benz was favourite after its 1954 successes plus Fangio's domination of the Argentinian Grand Prix and Juan Manuel and Moss both had special short chassis versions to cope with the particularities of the Monaco circuit. Backing them was supposed to be Hans Herrmann but the German had a big accident in practice and was replaced by Frenchman André Simon. Fangio added yet another pole to his tally with a lap in 1m 41.1s which Ascari equalled in his D 50 and Moss put himself on the outside of the front row by getting round in 1m 41.6s. On the second row were Castellotti and Behra while the third consisted of Villoresi, Mieres and Musso. Before the race Ascari exchanged his car with Chiron as the Italian had damaged his gearbox in practice. In the race the Monegasque, who was

• **130_** Monaco 22nd May 1955: Early on Eugenio Castellotti managed to get ahead of both Moss and Ascari. He came home 2nd in an eventful race.

• **131**_On the run down to the Station hairpin Ascari leads Castellotti who is followed by Jean Behra's 250 F Maserati. Little did Alberto know that this was to be his last Grand Prix.

taller than Ascari, found that the cockpit was too cramped for him and had to race with three speeds instead of five. The Lancia mechanics had to twist the gear lever on Chiron's car to prevent him from banging his knee on it.

The Grand Prix itself has remained rooted in racing legend for three main reasons: the rout of the Mercedes-Benz team, Ascari's dive into the harbour and Maurice Trintignant's unexpected though fully-deserved victory. Right from the start Fangio and Moss in their W 196s began to draw away form their pursuers led Ascari and Castellotti's Lancias and Behra's Maserati but this was not to be their day. On lap 25 Simon went out with an oil leak and then on lap 50 it was Fangio's turn to retire with blocked valves. This left Stirling Moss in the lead with a minute in hand over Ascari who was followed by Trintignant some thirty seconds back with Mieres on his heels. On lap 81 came another turn up for the books, as there was no sign of Moss! He had been hit by the

same problem as Fangio and it was later learnt that this was due to a rare error in the fitting of the valves in the Mercedes workshops. Suddenly the race was on again as Trintignant was pulling back two seconds a lap on Ascari now in the lead. Alberto did not know that Moss was out when he tackled the chicane for the eighty-first time. Suddenly a wheel locked and oil left by Moss's Mercedes sent the cherry red car into a spin: it ploughed through the fencing and plunged into the harbour. In that era there were no safety harnesses in F1. Ascari, who was a good swimmer and liked deep sea diving, got out of the large cockpit destined for Chiron without problems and came up to the surface within a few seconds. The frogmen stationed in the port in the event of just such an accident immediately rescued him. His Lancia was later pulled out of the water by a crane. Alberto, suffering from slight injuries to his face and nose and right thigh, was transported to the Monte Carlo hospital.

• **132**_ A huge cloud of spray is kicked up, as Alberto's's Lancia plunges into the Monaco harbour. Paul Frère passes in the Ferrari Squalo 555 he has taken over from Taruffi.
(Maniago collection)

• **133**_ The D 50 A is pulled out of the water by a crane. Ascari suffered only slight injuries and Trintignant, who won the race, went to see him in hospital for a chat.

Thus, Trintignant sped on to a totally unexpected victory, the first of his two world championship successes (the second was also in Monaco in 1958). For Ferrari it came out of the blue as Enzo knew that his cars were outclassed when he entered them for the Grand Prix.

Lancia also had reason to be satisfied. Despite Ascari's accident the Turin make scored a second place thanks to a good drive from Castellotti (who was catching Trintignant but ran out of time) and both Villoresi and Chiron finished in fifth and sixth positions. Overall, the Monaco race showed that the cars were progressing. All, however, was not well within the company. Gianni Lancia's decision to run a sports and F1 programme simultaneously – even if the

sports car part had been dropped for the 1955 season - had ruined his firm financially. Just at the very moment when the Lancias looked like they could beat the Mercedes-Benz a large question mark hung over their future. Would they be present at the next round of the championship, the Belgian Grand Prix?

Four days later came the final blow. On the morning of Thursday 26th May Ascari, who was back home in Milan having left the hospital on Tuesday without any apparent sequels following his accident, received a phone call from his friend Eugenio Castellotti. The latter was at Monza testing for the Supercortemaggiore Grand Prix the coming Sunday in which he was down to drive a 3-litres 4-cylinder 750 Monza Ferrari.

1955 Monaco Grand Prix
Lancia D50

P. MÉNARD

Designer: Vittorio Jano

Engine
Make/type: Lancia/D 50
No. of cylinders: 90° V8 (front, semi-stressed member)
Cubic capacity: 2488 ccs
Bore & stroke: 73.6 x 73.1 mm
Compression ratio: 12:1
Max. power: 255 bhp
Max. revs: 8200 rpm
Block: light alloy
Carburettors: 4 double choke Solex 40 P 11s
Distribution; 2x 2 D.O.H.Cs
No. of valves per cylinder: 2
Ignition: 2 magnetos
No. of plugs per cylinder: 2

Transmission
Gearbox/ no. of speeds: Lancia transversal unit with final drive, 5 + reverse
Clutch: Lancia hydraulic multi plate

Chassis
Type: small diameter tubular space frame
Suspension: independent, double wishbone, double torsion bar, transverse leaf springs/front, de Dion, rocker arm and transverse leaf springs/rear
Shock absorbers: Lancia telescopic
Wheels: Spoked Borranis
Tyres: 5.50 x 16 (Front) / 7.00 x 16 (Rear) Englebert
Brakes: outboard mounted drums all round

Dimensions
Wheelbase: 2280 mm
Tracks: 1294 mm (Front) / 1330 mm (Rear)
Fuel tanks' capacity: 200 litres
Dry weight: 620 kgs

Used in Spain in 1954, in Argentina and Monaco in 1955 and in 3 non-championship Grands Prix in 1955.

Ascari said he would come and watch the tests and after breakfast he dressed up in a suit and tie and told his wife he'd be back for lunch at one o'clock. He drove to the circuit without his racing equipment, his gloves and his famous blue helmet whose strap had been torn in his Monaco crash and was being repaired. Although he was down to drive in the race with Castellotti there was no reason for him to take part in this shakedown test. He arrived at the track at around 11h30 and had a chat with Castellotti and Count 'Johnny' Lurani over a cup of tea at the drivers' bar. Then in beautiful sunny weather they went to have a look at the new Ferrari, which still had unpainted bodywork. He said to his friends, "it's always better to get straight back into a car after an accident, isn't it?" He borrowed Castellotti's helmet, gloves and goggles, took off his jacket and stuffed his tie into his shirt. He checked the controls and said, 'I'd like to try her out to see if I'll be all right for Sunday. I'll only do a few laps slowly." He started, selected first gear, let out the clutch and drove off out onto the empty circuit. The 750 Ferrari he was driving for the first time was fitted with Englebert tyres and was a car which, both Mike Hawthorn and Paul Frère said, did not pardon the slightest mistake. Ascari did a warm up lap and then crossing the start/finish line speeded up. Third time round he went even quicker. He was never to complete the lap. In the Vialone corner, a fast right-hander that had been widened by the addition of an 80 metre long

(Archives Christian Bedel)

Maurice Trintignant: "One hell of a dive!"

"Ascari was bloody lucky. When I went to see him the next day I found him sitting in his bed sucking oranges! His radio was playing soft music. As it was hot he was nor wearing his pyjama top. I realised that we were wrong when we called him "fatty." He had a wrestler's powerful body, heavily muscled shoulders and a bull neck, strong biceps and forearms but without excess weight: in short he had exactly the right build for a rugby front row forward. He was not fat, he was a well-built athlete. He was in great form. If it hadn't been for the little bandage on his nose you'd never have thought that he'd had such a narrow escape. He held out his arms to me exclaiming with a laugh, 'come here till I congratulate you, you old bastard!' ... I'm really delighted about your win... but still if I went for a swim it's your fault! Would you believe that since the sixty-eighth lap my brakes were playing up. Each time my front wheels locked. It was very tiring as the car went sideways in every corner. I managed to control it but my pit told me that you were pulling back over two seconds a lap! I was second behind Moss and I knew I couldn't catch him but I wanted to hang on to my place in case anything happened to the Mercedes. To stop you catching me I had to take risks. As bad luck would have it I skidded in the chicane. I slid on oil and I hit the pavement. The result was that I found myself heading for the sea and I couldn't do anything about it because my front wheels were locked. And splash! I fell into the water with the car but I managed to get out just as we were going down. It was one hell of a dive and I hit the bottom. I was a bit stunned but the coolness of the water woke me up. When I came to the surface a frogman was already there to pick me up, luckily for me!" 'Extract from: "Pilote de Course" by Maurice Trintignant.

• **135_** Monza 26th May 1955: The wrecked Ferrari Monza after Ascari's accident. *(Maniago collection)*

• **136**_ Milan 28th May 1955: Ascari's funeral. His coffin is carried out of the San Carlo chapel by among others, his friends Villoresi on the left and Castellotti on the right. *(Maniago collection)*

strip of asphalt, the Ferrari slid, then snapped sideways and escaped its driver's control. It rolled over and over and screeched to a halt on the left-hand side of the track. The driver was thrown out. Suddenly a deadly hush fell over the Autodromo. Lurani and Villoresi ran to the scene where they found Ascari lying on the grass verge: he was very badly injured with multiple fractures. He was then stretchered to an ambulance in which he died in the arms of his great friend Villoresi on the way to hospital.

At number 60 Corso Sampione in the Ascari household Mietta, together with her children, was waiting for her husband to return for lunch. A friend told her that he had had a bad accident and she was taken to the chapel of the Monza

hospital in which Alberto was lying. He was a very superstitious man. The date of his accident was 26th May and he was seven weeks off his thirty-seventh birthday. His father had been killed on the 26th July at the same age.

The whole of Italy shared the Ascari family's grief. Alberto had become a true national hero like Fausto Coppi and Tazio Nuvolari for the previous generation. When his coffin was being transported from Monza to Milan people massed on either side of the road to pay their final respects. The religious ceremony for his funeral was held on Saturday 28th May, two days after his accident, in the San Carlo al Corso chapel, in his Milan parish. His coffin was carried by Castellotti, Villoresi and Maglioli among others. ∎

Epilogue
1955... Nobody to fill his shoes

• **137**_ Reims 1st July 1956: The D 50 Lancias were transformed into Lancia-Ferraris for the 1956 season. Peter Collins started from pole in n°.14 ahead of Castellotti in n°.12 and that was how they finished in the A.C.F Grand Prix.

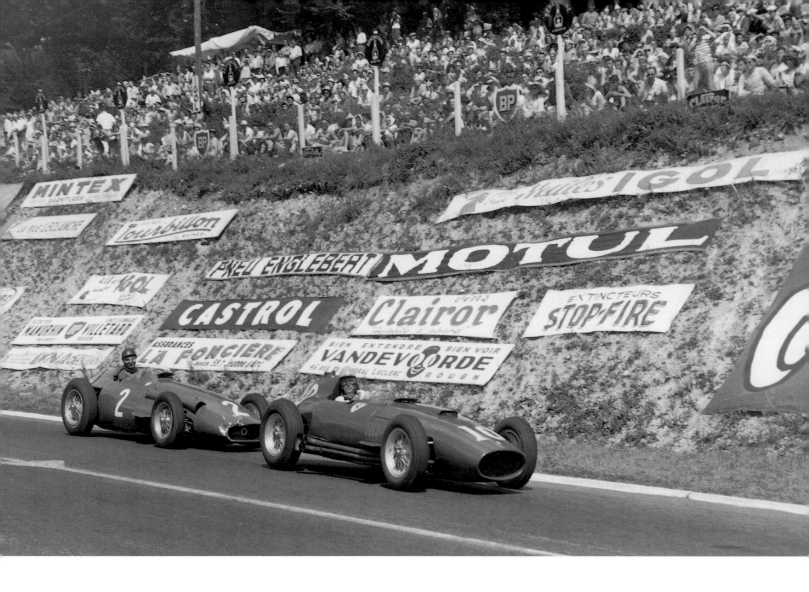

The causes of Ascari's fatal accident will never be known. Was it due to the sequels of his Monaco crash, defective tyres, a mechanical problem on his Ferrari? Several hypotheses have been put forward but none has been irrefutably proved. However, the show went on. In Turin where the financial situation of the Lancia Company was in a catastrophic state Gianni Lancia, Vittorio Jano and their collaborators, completely devastated by the accident, wanted to stop everything immediately. However, Castellotti persuaded them to send a car to Belgium in homage to Ascari's memory. In practice for the Grand Prix the young Italian put in a blindingly quick lap to claim pole in 4m 18.1s from Fangio's Mercedes-Benz which got round in 4m 18.6s and Moss in 4m 19.2s. In the race itself he managed to hang on to the two German cars until the gearbox gave up the ghost on lap 17. Not long afterwards came the Le Mans tragedy in which over eighty people died and more than a hundred were injured. Among the direct

consequences of the accident was the cancellation of the French, German and Swiss Grands Prix. In the meantime Gianni Lancia had decided to stop his racing programme. He began discussions with other constructors via the Italian Automobile Club to find a buyer for his cars. Maserati refused then Ferrari did the same out of pride even though Enzo too was in deep trouble. He changed his mind when the Federation came up with a 50 millions lira offer - which came from Fiat in fact - in an attempt to relaunch Italian motor racing at the highest level. And so on 26th July he got his hands on the complete Lancia F1 team made up of six D 50s, several engines and a large stock of spares plus Vittorio Jano who joined the Ferrari design office.

The Italian Grand Prix on 11ᵗʰ September on the Monza circuit saw Ferrari enter three 555 Super Squalos plus four Lancia D 50s for Farina, Castellotti and Villoresi who qualified on the second and third rows behind the Mercedes-Benz. They non-started, however, due to a tyre problem although Ferrari gave Castellotti a car for the Grand Prix. On 24th September a pair were entered for the Gold Cup on the Oulton park circuit. Mike Hawthorn finished second behind Moss's 250 F Maserati and Castellotti came home seventh. This was the last appearance of the Lancia D 50 in its original form. In 1956, they were modified and designated Lancia-Ferraris and enabled Fangio to win his fourth F1 World Championship title. In addition, Musso and Castellotti fought a few memorable duels in them notably at Monza which, albeit briefly, inspired fresh hope in the *Tifosi's* bosom that a successor to the late great Ascari had been found.

Alas, this was not to be the case. Veterans Farina and Villoresi gave up racing in 1956. Eugenio Castellotti, Ascari's protégé, died in private practice on the Modena autodromo in March 1957 and in July 1958 Luigi Musso was killed in a high-speed accident on the Reims circuit in the French Grand Prix. Three years later on the same circuit 27-year-old Giancarlo Baghetti scored a totally unexpected victory in a Ferrari 156 before disappearing into the dustbins of history despite a few successes in endurance and sports car racing. The next Italian to mark the Grand Prix scene was Lorenzo Bandini. He was born in 1935 and made a name for himself

• **139**_ Reims 6th July 1958: At the start of the French Grand Prix Harry Schell's BRM and Tony Brooks' Vanwall get the better of the Dino Ferraris driven by Luigi Musso (n°.2) and Mike Hawthorn (n°.4). Musso was killed on lap 10.

• 140_ Reims 2nd July 1961: The nail biting finish to the French Grand Prix which Baghetti won by a whisker from Dan Gurney's Porsche. It was the Italian's only F1 World Championship victory.

• 141_ Silverstone 8th July 1961: Before the start of the British Empire Trophy double world champion Jack Brabham (1959-60) is at the wheel of a Sunbeam Alpine about to do a presentation lap. His passengers are Juan Manuel Fangio (world champion in 1951-54-55-56-57) and in the back 19-year-old Tonino Ascari, Alberto's son who tried his hand at racing with Cooper but without success.

thanks to his serious approach to racing and his very pleasant personality. He began in Formula Junior with the Scuderia Centro-Sud and his first drives in F1 were in a Cooper-Maserati and a BRM. In 1962 he was taken on by Ferrari and was the protégé of the new team manager, Eugenio Dragoni who did everything he could (and sometimes more) to further his career. In 1964, Bandini won the Austrian Grand Prix on the Zeltweg circuit and like Baghetti it was his only world championship victory. He was a good co-driver and a skilled test driver but his career came to a horrible end in a fiery accident in his 312 F1 on the Monaco circuit in 1967 where he had finished second in 1965 and 1966.

In 1963, the Scuderia took on another endurance specialist, Ludovico Scarfiotti, winner of the 1963 Le Mans 24 Hours with Bandini in a 250 P Ferrari. Out of a total of ten Grands Prix seven were in a Ferrari and he won the 1966 Italian Grand Prix in a 312 F1 giving fresh hope to the Italians after John Surtees's walkout the same year which was dominated by Jack Brabham's

● **142_** *Zeltweg 23rd August 1964: Lorenzo Bandini scored his only F1 Grand Prix victory in the Austrian round in his F1 158 Ferrari after many of the favourites fell by the wayside.*

Brabhams. Scarfiotti did not win another Grand Prix and continued his prototype career specialising in hill climbs. After winning the European Hill Climbing Championship for Ferrari he signed with Porsche for the 1968 season and in June of that year he was killed when his Porsche spyder crashed in the Rossfeld hill climb in Germany.

In the 70s two other Italians, Ignazio Giunti, killed in Buenos Aires in a sports car race, and Arturo Merzario briefly entertained the illusion of an Italian revival in the Scuderia Ferrari, which at that moment was going through a period of turmoil. Little 'Art' did not convince in a couple of seasons apart from a few good performances in the 312 PB sports car and continued his career elsewhere.

No summary would be complete without mentioning Mario Andretti who also drove for Ferrari in 1971-72 and 1982 without ever doing a full season. He was born in 1940 and was a great admirer of Alberto Ascari whom he had seen in action at Monza in 1954 just before his family emigrated to the USA. Enzo had a lot of respect for Andretti and the Italo-American won the

• **143_** Monza 4th September 1966: Following John Surtees' abrupt departure from Ferrari Lodovico Scarfiotti, better known as a prototype and endurance specialist, joined the Scuderia. Starting behind Mike Parkes he gave Ferrari a win in its home Grand Prix in his 12-cylinder 312 and also set the fastest lap.

• **144_** Kyalami 6th March 1971: Italian born Mario Andretti domiciled in the USA is seen here ahead of the BRMs driven by Pedro Rodriguez (n°.16) and Jo Siffert (n°.17). Mario, who was a great admirer of Ascari, went on to win the race but his F1 World Championship title came at the wheel of a Lotus in 1978.

1971 South African Grand Prix in a Ferrari. But Mario decided to pursue his career in the United States where he built up a formidable string of successes in Indy Cars, Formula 5000, CanAm and stock cars as well as winning the 1978 F1 World Championship in the Lotus 79.

In the 1980s Italy seemed to have found its successor to Ascari in the elegant and urbane Michele Alboreto. He was born in Milan on 23rd December 1956 and made his debut in the Tyrrell team when he was not yet twenty-five. He stayed with Tyrrell for three seasons and scored two wins for the once great English squad, Las Vegas in 1982 and Detroit in 1983, Tyrrell's last F1 Grand Prix victory. In 1984, Michele joined the Scuderia and took on the turbocharged BMW-engined Brabhams, McLaren-TAG Porsches and Renaults. In 1985, he was Prost's most serious rival for the world championship title after winning the Canadian and German Grands Prix but he was let down by his car. Perhaps too he lacked the calculating ability of the Frenchman and the aggressiveness of Senna and his best result in F1 was runner up in 1985 with 53 points. He stayed with the Scuderia until 1988 and then his career went steadily downhill after half-a-season with Tyrrell in 1989 as he was thrown out in favour of Jean Alesi. He retired from the F1 scene in 1994 after having driven for tail-enders like Arrows, Footwork, Lola and Minardi. He then competed in Super Touring Cars and Sports Prototypes (winning Le Mans in a TWR-Porsche in 1997). He was killed testing an Audi prototype on the Lausitring on 25th April 2001. He will be remembered as a great driver and a very charming human being who inspired the *Tifosi* in the mid-eighties. Ferrari still continues to nourish Italy's dreams but as yet no italian driver has really replaced Ascari. The unforgettable. ∎

• **145_** Zolder 29th April 1984: Michael Alboreto in the no.27 126/C4 Ferrari won the Belgian Grand Prix from Warwick's Renault and Arnoux's Ferrari. He was the Tifosi's last hope of an Italian F1 World Champion at the wheel of a Ferrari.

_STATISTICS

Ascari raced in about 200 events – motorbikes excluded – in his all too brief career. In keeping with the schema of the Collection "Formula 1 Legends" the reader will find his F1 World Championship results in the 32 Grands Prix in which he raced between 1950 and 1955. It will be seen that the Italian champion's 13 victories give him a success rate of just over 40% putting him in second place overall behind Juan Manuel Fangio (24 wins in 49 Grands Prix, almost 49%). He is ahead of Michael Schumacher who, with 83 victories in 212 Grands Prix at the end of the 2004 season, has a strike rate of 39%. The German is the only driver since Fangio capable of overtaking Ascari in terms of percentage.

After the world championship tables the reader will find a list of Ascari's main wins in non-championship F1 and F2 races (plus those not counting for the 1952-53 championship) as well as his victories in F. Libre and Sports Car events. ■

FORMULA 1_THE 32 GRANDS PRIX

1950_

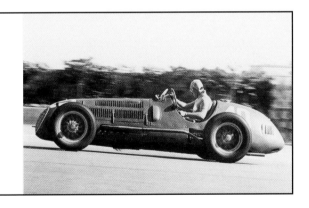

GRAND PRIX	DATE	CIRCUIT	CAR	QUALIFYING	RACE
1. Monaco	21 May	Monaco	Ferrari 125 C	7th (1'54"8)	2nd
2. Switzerland	4 June	Berne-Bremgarten	Ferrari 125 C	5th (2'46"8)	Rtd (oil)
3. Belgium	18 June	Spa-Francorchamps	Ferrari 275 F1	6th (4'49")	5th
4. Italy	3 September	Monza	Ferrari 375 F1	2nd (1'58"4)	2nd *

(*) Italy: after taking over Serafini's car
Position in World Championship: 5th / 11 points
Average points per race for season: 2.75

1951_

GRAND PRIX	DATE	CIRCUIT	CAR	QUALIFYING	RACE
1. Switzerland	27 May	Berne-Bremgarten	Ferrari 375 F1	7th (2.460)	6th
2. Belgium	17 June	Spa-Francorchamps	Ferrari 375 F1	4th (4.300)	2nd
3. ACF/Europe	1st July	Reims-Gueux	Ferrari 375 F1	3rd (2:28.100)	2nd*
4. Great Britain	14 July	Silverstone	Ferrari 375 F1	4th (1:45.400)	Rtd (gearbox)
5. Germany	29 July	Nürburgring	Ferrari 375 F1	**Pole (9:55.800)**	1st
6. Italy	16 September	Monza	Ferrari 375 F1	3rd (1:55.100)	**1st**
7. Spain	28 October	Barcelone-Pedralbes	Ferrari 375 F1	**Pole (2:10.590)**	4th

(*) ACF: 2nd after taking over Gonzalez's car.

Position in World Championship: 2nd / 28 points (25 retained)
2 poles, 2 victories
Average points per race for season: 4

1952_

GRAND PRIX	DATE	CIRCUIT	CAR	QUALIFYING	RACE
1. Indy 500 *	30 May	Indianapolis	Ferrari 375 F1	21st (216.147)	Rtd (wheel)
2. Belgium/Europe	22 June	Spa-Francorchamps	Ferrari 500 F2	**Pole (4:37.000)**	**1st FRL**
3. ACF	6 July	Rouen-les-Essarts	Ferrari 500 F2	**Pole (2:14.800)**	**1st FRL**
4. Great Britain	19 July	Silverstone	Ferrari 500 F2	2nd (1:50.000)	**1st FRL**
5. Germany	3rd August	Nürburgring	Ferrari 500 F2	**Pole (10:04.900)**	**1st FRL**
6. Holland	17 August	Zandvoort	Ferrari 500 F2	**Pole (1:46.500)**	**1st FRL**
7. Italy	7 September	Monza	Ferrari 500 F2	**Pole (2:05.700)**	**1st FRL****

(*) Ascari gave the Swiss GP a miss to race in the Indianapolis 500 Miles. He was the only driver to compete in this race which counted for the world championship and that is why it is included in his total of 32. Between 1950 and 1960 no Indy driver raced in a Grand Prix. Except Troy Ruttman (ACF 1958) and Rodger Ward (USA 1959).
(**) Shared with Gonzalez's Maserati.

Position in World Championship:
World Champion / 36 Points out of 53.5 scored
5 poles, 6 victories, 6 fastest race laps (FRL)
Average per race: 7.64 (excluding Indianapolis 8.9166 !)

1953_

GRAND PRIX	DATE	CIRCUIT	CAR	QUALIFYING	RACE
1. Argentina	18 January	Buenos Aires	Ferrari 500 F2	**Pole (1:49.000)**	**1st FRL**
2. Holland	7 June	Zandvoort	Ferrari 500 F2	**Pole (1:51.100)**	**1st**
3. Belgium	21 June	Spa-Francorchamps	Ferrari 500 F2	2nd (4:32.000)	**1st**
4. ACF	5 July	Reims-Gueux	Ferrari 500 F2	**Pole (2:41.200)**	4th FRL*
5. Great Britain	18 July	Silverstone	Ferrari 500 F2	**Pole (1:48.000)**	**1st FRL****
6. Germany	2nd August	Nürburgring	Ferrari 500 F2	**Pole (9:59.800)**	8th ***
7. Switzerland	23 August	Berne-Bremgarten	Ferrari 500 F2	2nd (2:40.700)	**1st FRL**
8. Italy	13 September	Monza	Ferrari 500 F2	**Pole (2:02.700)**	Rtd (accident)

(*) Shared with Fangio (Maserati).
(**) Shared with Gonzalez (Maserati).
(***) Took over Villoresi's car.

Position in World Championship:
World Champion / 34.5 Points out of 47 scored
6 poles, 5 victories, 4 fastest race laps (FRL)
Average points per race for season: 5.875

1954_

GRAND PRIX	DATE	CIRCUIT	CAR	QUALIFYING	RACE
1. ACF	4 July	Reims-Gueux	Maserati 250 F	3rd (2:30.500)	Rtd (clutch)
2. Great Britain	17 July	Silverstone	Maserati 250 F	(no time*)	Rtd (engine) **FRL****
3. Italy	5 September	Monza	Ferrari 625 F1	2nd (1:59.200)	Rtd. (engine)
4. Spain	24 October	Barcelone-Pedr.	Lancia D 50	**Pole (2:18.500)**	Rtd (clutch) **FRL**

(*) The Maseratis arrived too late for timed practice. The regulations of the era allowed them to start from the back of the grid. Ascari was 28th out of 31.
(**) He shared it with Gonzalez (Ferrari), Moss (Maserati), Fangio (Mercedes-Benz), Hawthorn (Ferrari), Behra (Gordini) and Marimon (Maserati) so no point was awarded.

Position in World Championship: 25th / 1 point
1 pole, 2 fastest race laps
Average points per race for season: 0.25

1955_

GRAND PRIX	DATE	CIRCUIT	CAR	QUALIFYING	RACE
1. Argentina	16 January	Buenos Aires	Lancia D 50	2nd (1:43.200)	Rtd (accident)
2. Monaco/Europe	22 May	Monaco	Lancia D 50	2nd (1:41.100)	Rtd (accident)

Position in World Championship: non-classified.

NON-CHAMPIONSHIP FORMULA 1 VICTORIES

1948

COUNTRY	DATE	RACE	CIRCUIT	CAR	
I	27 June	San Remo GP	Ospedaletti	Maserati 4 CLT	

1949

CH	3rd July	Swiss GP	Berne-Bremgarten	Ferrari 125 C	
G-B	20 August	International Trophy	Silverstone	Ferrari 125 C	**FRL**
I	11 September	Italian/European GP	Monza	Ferrari 125 C	**FRL**

1950

E	29 October	Penya Rhin GP	Barcelone-Pedralbes	Ferrari 375 F1	**FRL**

1951

I	22 April	San Remo GP	Ospedaletti	Ferrari 375 F1	**FRL**

1955

I	27 March	Turin GP	Parc Valentino	Lancia D 50	
I	8 May	Naples GP	Posillipo	Lancia D 50	

NON-CHAMPIONSHIP F2 VICTORIES

1949

COUNTRY	DATE	RACE	CIRCUIT	CAR
F	17 July	J-P Wimille Cup	Reims-Gueux	Ferrari 166 F2
I	4 September	Bari GP	Lungomare	Ferrari 166 F2
L	?	Luxemburg GP	Luxembourg	Ferrari 166 F2

1950

I	7 May	Modena GP	Autodromo	Ferrari 166 F2
I	11 June	Rome GP	Caracalla	Ferrari 166 F2
F	2nd July	J-P Wimille Cup	Reims-Gueux	Ferrari 166 F2
D	20 August	German GP	Nürburgring	Ferrari 166 F2
I	15 October	Garde Circuit	Salo	Ferrari 166 F2

1951

I	13 May	Monza GP	Monza	Ferrari 166 F2
I	24 June	Naples GP	Posillipo	Ferrari 166 F2
I	23 September	Modena GP	Autodromo	Ferrari 500 F2

1952

I	16 March	Syracuse GP	Syracuse	Ferrari 500 F2
F	14 April	Pau GP	Parc Beaumont	Ferrari 500 F2
F	27 April	Marseille GP	Parc Borély	Ferrari 500 F2
I	8 June	Autodromo GP	Monza	Ferrari 500 F2
F	10 August	Comminges GP	Saint-Gaudens	Ferrari 500 F2*
F	28 August	La Baule GP	La Baule-Escoublac	Ferrari 500 F2

*Took over André Simon's car.

1953

F	22 March	Pau GP	Parc Beaumont	Ferrari 500 F2
F	3 May	Bordeaux GP	Bordeaux	Ferrari 500 F2

FORMULA LIBRE VICTORIES

1949

COUNTRY	DATE	RACE	CIRCUIT	CAR
ARG	29 January	Buenos Aires GP	Parc Palermo	Maserati 4 CLT

1950

COUNTRY	DATE	RACE	CIRCUIT	CAR
ARG	8 January	Buenos Aires GP	Parc Palermo	Ferrari 166 C
ARG	15 January	Mae del Plata GP	El Torreon	Ferrari 166 C

SPORTS CAR VICTORIES

1947

COUNTRY	DATE	RACE	CIRCUIT	CAR
I	28 September	Modena GP	Autodromo	Maserati A 6 GCS

1948

COUNTRY	DATE	RACE	CIRCUIT	CAR
I	15 August	Pescara Circuit	Pescara	Maserati A 6 GCS

1950

COUNTRY	DATE	RACE	CIRCUIT	CAR
L	3rd May	Luxemburg GP	Luxembourg	Ferrari 166 MM
G.-B.	26 August	Daily Express Trophy	Silverstone	Ferrari 166 MM

1953

COUNTRY	DATE	RACE	CIRCUIT	CAR
D	30 August	ADAC 1000 kms	Nürburgring	Ferrari 375 MM*

*Co-driver: Nino Farina

1954

COUNTRY	DATE	RACE	CIRCUIT	CAR
I	1st - 2nd May	Mille Miglia	Brescia-Rome-Brescia	Lancia D 24

ABREVIATIONS_

Rtd: Retired
ARG: Argentina
CH: Switzerland
D: Germany
E: Spain
F: France
FRL: Fastest lap
GB: Great Britain
I: Italy
L: Luxemburg

The 1953 Italian Grand Prix: Ascari (n°.4 Ferrari) is shown here during his titanic duel with Fangio (n°.50 Maserati), Farina (n°.6 Ferrari) and Marimon (n°. 54 Maserati). It all ended in tears for the reigning World Champion.

INDEX

_ACKNOWLEDGEMENTS

Christian Bedeï, Adriano Cimarosti, Cyril Davillerd, Maria Teresa De Filippis, Michel Delannoy, Luc Domenjoz, Christian Huet, Louis Klemantaski, Christian Moity, Barbara Premoli, Jean Sage, Maurice Trintignant and Sylvie Vassal.

_BIBLIOGRAPHY

"Antonio e Alberto Ascari", by Cesare de Agostini - L'Éditrice Automobile, Milan, 1968;
"Alberto Ascari - Ferrari's first double champion", by Karl Ludvigsen - Haynes Publishing, London, 2000;
«"Piloti, che gente", by Enzo Ferrari - E.P.A., Paris 1987;
"The roaring races - The true story of Enzo Ferrari race car driver", by Giulio Schmidt - Libreria Automobile, Milan, 1988;
"Fangio - cuando el hombre es mas que el mito", by Juan Manuel Fangio and Roberto Carozzo, Sudamericana Planeta, Buenos Aires, 1986;
"Challenge me the race", by Mike Hawthorn - Aston Publications, London, 1958;
"Pilote de courses", by Maurice Trintignant - Hachette, Paris, 1957;
"Historique de la course automobile", by Edmond Cohin - Éditions Larivière, Paris 1978;
"Les Grands Prix de Formule 1 hors Championnat du Monde", by Christian Naviaux - Éditions du Palmier, Nîmes, 2002;
"Mille Miglia 1927-1957", by Giovanni Lurani - Edita Vilo, Lausanne, 1979.